Claire
A mother's journey from infertility to love

CLAIRE DE JAGER

· PUBLISHING ·

www.africanperspectives.co.za

African Perspectives Publishing
PO Box 95342, Grant Park 2051,
Johannesburg, South Africa
www.africanperspectives.co.za

© Claire de Jager

All rights reserved

No part of this publication may be reproduced, stored in a retrieval system or transmitted in any form or by any means, electronic, mechanical, photocopying or otherwise,
without the prior permission of the author.

ISBN PRINT: 978-1-0370-0867-2
ISBN DIGITAL: 978-1-0370-0837-5

Editor: Richard Gibbs
Proofreader: Rose Francis
Typesetter: Phumzile Mondlani
Cover Image: Angelique Blignaut
Cover Design: Jenilee Prinsloo - Ryzenberg

Dedication

To Joshua, Mikey and Katie

Mom and Dad walked the darkest valley as we struggled to have children, but we would do it all again if it meant getting you precious three. You have made our journey worthwhile. We wouldn't choose to have our family any other way. You are our miracle children!

Contents

LIFE IS TO BE LIVED 7

A MATCH MADE IN HEAVEN 25

GOD'S GRACE IN SILENT DESPAIR 37

CHANGING PERSPECTIVES: 61

GOING AGAINST THE GRAIN OF TRADITION 61

A LEAP OF FAITH 103

THE WONDER THAT IS OUR BOYS 117

JOY COMPLETE 135

NAVIGATING FAMILY DYNAMICS 151

CULTIVATED BY LOVE 159

YOUTHFUL PERSPECTIVE 167

EPILOGUE 173

RESOURCES 175

ACKNOWLEDGEMENTS 177

LIFE IS TO BE LIVED

Growing up as a white South African

I was born privileged into a white, English-speaking family in South Africa in 1974. The colour of my skin, entitled me to a good education, a home in the suburbs, and many opportunities South Africans born with darker skin did not have.

We were taught Apartheid was wrong, but we had never experienced anything different. We grew up in white schools and had no teachers or classmates of colour. I remember a girl in our class telling us about her friend who was the daughter of their domestic worker. It was such a foreign concept, as none of us knew children that were not white - and we were not going to meet them where we grew up.

My Mom did not work for most of my childhood, so we had the privilege of having her at home with us every afternoon after school. Money wasn't an issue as my Dad earned well. Mabel was our helper, and Gladman our gardener's mother. She could not read. She interpreted pictures in the newspapers to my Mom of what she thought was happening in the World. When she was first able to vote in 1994, she said she would not vote unless she could vote for my father, who was not a politician.

I remember being in high school when our school first accepted a student that was not white. I never met her because I was too shy to speak to her. I wondered at her bravery and what it was like being the only person of colour in a school of 1,200 learners.

My family placed much emphasis on education. My parents had degrees, even my grandmother had been to university. It was an accepted norm that we would obtain a tertiary education and choose what we wanted to study.

When I attended university, there were several people of colour staying in residence which made it easy to get to know everyone. Although I had not grown up knowing anyone of colour, it seemed completely normal studying, laughing, having fun, and completing assignments together. Friendships were built. But it was also the first time we began to hear what it was like living in South Africa if you were not white. The unnecessary injustice of it all. The realisation that a minority could create so much pain and suffering for so many.

My childhood was easy in terms of what I had and the opportunities afforded to me, yet I struggled with self-esteem for years. I felt scared, almost threatened, by most people. I was worried other children, or their parents would not like me. I was far too scared to just start a conversation with someone. I kept to myself and flew under the radar where I felt safe. It meant I did not have many playdates and spent most of my childhood playing with my younger brother or reading. I tried hard not to be noticed at school, to avoid getting into trouble. I even had nightmares about being shouted at by our short-tempered headmaster.

By the time I reached high school, I was so self-conscious, it felt like I might have forgotten how to walk. Every morning, walking into school, I would wonder if I had an uneven gait or if it looked like I was walking uncomfortably. I would try to remind myself to walk 'left leg - right leg' to appear normal. Finding certain subjects difficult to comprehend also made me feel more visible. But so was eating at breaktime. I did not want to chew in public in case everyone looked at me.

I loathed going shopping after school and walking through the shopping mall in my school uniform as I felt it made me recognisable. I was so self-conscious that someone might see me and recognise me. I have no idea where that fear originated from, but my confidence was sorely lacking. Some days after school, my Mom would stop by the shops to buy bread rolls for lunch. Our post box was near the shops, so she would ask one of us to pop out to get the rolls and the other, to fetch the post. I always fetched the post right up until Grade 11, when I was asked specifically to buy the rolls. I refused.

My family did not notice that I did not approach the checkout. I felt so self - conscious standing there in the queue not knowing what to do with my hands that I would select what was needed and give it to my confident younger sister to approach the checkout. When Mom recognised this fear, she ordered my older brother to accompany me into the shop to ensure I stood in the queue and paid for what I purchased at the checkout.

My university years

Somehow, university was different. I felt I could make real connections. Like I fitted in – I belonged. I had so much fun and felt a sense of freedom from the fear I had endured for so long. I felt I could trust just being me, and by the end of our first year of studies, my roommate and I received an award for the Most Dynamic First Year Students. Imagine!

I always wanted to play netball but was never brave enough except for three weeks in Grade 5 when I attended practice. All the popular girls played netball, so I spent three weeks watching how to play the game. My fingernails suffered the anguish as I would spend the whole time biting them out of nervousness and a distinct feeling that the other girls believed I should not be there. So, I left.

At varsity, our team could not play unless they had enough players. I was their missing piece. If I was willing to be a part of the team when they were short of a player, they could play. After arriving at matches, I would receive a quick explanation of the position I would be playing – which meant nothing to me – then an explanation of where I would stand, which lines I could move between and what my role in that position was. If the whistle blew as a result of me doing something wrong, a teammate would inconspicuously approach me to let me know what I had done wrong and what the corrective action was - and the game would continue. No judgment, just inclusion and fun.

Studying my course of choice was complicated as I did not receive the required marks. This resulted in me having to start my first year with a BA degree and then reapplying for the course I wanted to study. After the first year, I reapplied for my course of choice and again, I was not accepted. This left me with a tough decision as the university only allowed us to apply for a new course after our first year or our final year. I did not want just a BA degree, so I decided to apply for Social Work. My Dad had been very successful with a BA degree, so he could not understand why I opposed it. My Mom told me my grandfather would 'turn in his grave' if I studied Social Work because of the emotional turmoil it could cause.

Nonetheless, I felt it was what I needed to do. The challenge started when the application form stated I needed a teacher to complete specific questions about my personality and community involvement. This was difficult for two reasons. The first was that I had been out of school for a year already, and the second was that having flown under the radar at school, the teachers did not know me, except for one who was no longer employed at the school.

I faxed the form to my Dad's office and then phoned to let him know, as I knew he and Mom were leaving shortly for an overseas trip. Unfortunately, Dad told me he had already left the office. They were about to take my brother to a friend's house to stay whilst they were away, then drive to the airport for a two-week vacation.

My application had to be returned to the university in three weeks, and it had to be posted – it could not be faxed back. My world felt like it was crumbling ... but God is always in control. The caretaker at my Dad's place of work, decided he would like to surprise my parents by fetching and taking them to the airport. He thought he would double-check my Dad's office to ensure he hadn't left anything behind, when he came across my fax. He arrived at my parent's home, fax in hand, and my brother was given the fax and asked to take it to school to ask any teacher who remembered me to complete it and post it to the university.

Boy, was I surprised when he contacted me the following day to let me know that the only teacher who knew me was at the school visiting that Monday. He gave her the fax, which she completed and sent to the university on time.

First-year Social Work was a challenge because it was not what I had chosen to do, but what I felt I had to do to get a professional qualification. Although I completed all my necessary assignments, I was not motivated or excited about this new course of study. However, I completed the year and came fourth academically in the class. By the end of the year, I started to enjoy my course and decided I wanted to continue with it.

No matter how hard I worked over the next three years, I never reached the top half of the class again. It was as though God carried me while convincing me of what I needed to do and stepped back once I made the decision and took responsibility for it.

For one of our practical placements, I asked Mom to pray that I would get to work with older or disabled people. The other category option I had was to work with children. I did not want to be placed with them as they made me feel self-conscious. I just did not feel I could work with children.

When our placements were announced, I was placed with children. I was anxious about it, and when I spoke to Mom, who said God answered prayers, I realised my Mom felt I would be good with children.

I was out of my comfort zone when I started, but the further I proceeded, the more I enjoyed working with children. I could never have imagined that play therapy would be a profession offered in South Africa and that I would have the opportunity to study short courses in this discipline during my undergraduate degree.

I absolutely loved it and decided I needed to study for a master's degree in play therapy. But first, I wanted to travel overseas and work as a social worker.

After graduating with a degree in social work, I decided to travel overseas to gain work experience and see the world. I did not know what area of social work I wanted to specialise in, but I knew I would never work in child protection. Yet this was precisely the area of social work God had planned for me over the next four years. Having decided, I booked an air ticket to the UK and left a month after graduating. The plan was to find employment, save pounds, and get to Camp America the same year.

Excited to arrive in the UK

Arriving alone in the UK was nerve-wracking and was made more so when upon arriving at Heathrow airport, I was sent from terminal one to three in search of obtaining x-rays of my chest to ensure I did not have tuberculosis. Only then was I allowed to enter the UK.

I had several interviews set up with different agencies for work, so I was very excited. I had wonderful ideas for working with children in little villages in the UK. My interviews were all in big cities and numerous boroughs in London, Southampton, Manchester, Birmingham and Peterborough. I remember leaving an interview with an agency whose offices were on Buckingham Palace Road asking where Buckingham Palace was in relation to where we were. I marvelled at how close I was to this iconic symbol of British monarchy and grandeur.

After a few weeks of being in the UK, I headed off to Bristol to visit my family. I arrived before they were home. There were no big bushes in the garden for me to hide my backpack. I decided to put it out of sight behind a fence and took my book to read on the Downs. From a distance, I spotted the Bristol (Avon) bridge and had to take a closer look. Two hours later, my aunt and cousin enthusiastically greeted me at the door and ushered me inside. I was cold.

I secured a job outside of London and moved there. As a duty social worker, I assessed information through phone calls and visiting clients. It was a steep learning curve. For every client that phoned in, we had a specific form to complete. One part of the form was to note the ethnicity of the callers. We were told that we should just ask the callers directly. I felt I could not do this if someone phoned in a crisis; it would sound like I had no compassion if I then asked their ethnicity. So, I based it on how they sounded. In South Africa, we can often tell by people's accents whether they are black or white. Well, you can imagine my shock when a family I described as being white arrived to meet with me, and they were black. Yip! That was a swift lesson in ethnicity and how easily we tend to 'box' people into our preconceived ideas on race.

I learnt very quickly that although the proper dress code for a social work student at an Afrikaans university is to always have your shoulders and waist covered and to wear long skirts or pants, this was different in the UK. One morning, as I walked past my manager, he told me I reminded him of a curtain because of my skirts.

Off to America

After working for eight months in the UK, I headed to Camp America. I was so excited to visit another country and work at a children's camp. We had to arrive a week earlier than the children to receive training because this camp was a special needs camp. We also had to unlearn certain European ways so that we did not pass them on to American children.

We learnt that 'you're welcome' was the accepted response to a child thanking us, not 'it's a pleasure.' Knives at the table are used for cutting food and then are to be placed on the table. Forks are then used to scoop food and eat it, with no balancing food on the back of forks.

Different coloured swimming caps conveyed the special needs of each child. Yellow indicated the child had hearing difficulties, blue indicated heart problems, and red - seizures.

If children were diagnosed with more than one of these special needs, red caps would surpass the blue or yellow, and blue caps would surpass the yellow.

We had to unpack the children's bags and make their beds with their bedding so that when they arrived, they would recognise their belongings and feel safe and secure. The training was fascinating, and the children were awesome.

Although I can't describe it as fun, one of my memories was standing in the bathroom with three little girls, waiting for the shower water to heat. I had my hand under the flow of water as I waited for it to reach the right temperature. It was still quite cool on my hand, yet I felt warm water flowing over my foot.

When I looked down, one of the girls was peeing on my foot, seemingly obliviously, while waiting to shower.

After the camp, our visas allowed us to travel America for a month. All the camp counsellors were dispatched in New York and travelled from there. Kylie, my Australian roommate and I decided to travel together.

One of the places we visited was Albany. We arrived late at night. The management left the door unlocked with arrows along the passages and staircases on pieces of paper guiding us to our bedroom. How different this was from South Africa, where it would be unheard of to have people in your home in the middle of the night unattended with the doors unlocked.

At the breakfast table the following morning, we met our hostess and two other South Africans who were also lodging there. Imagine my surprise when we asked them where they were from – one was from my suburb and attended the same school as I. I was shocked when I asked her what her surname was. I immediately recognised it. Our moms were friends, and as little kids in primary school, we played together and visited each other's homes.

Just before arriving at Niagara Falls, I received an email from my Mom letting me know that a family friend had passed away and that my Dad had bought his four-wheel drive vehicle from him just before he passed. John and I had always joked about me 'inheriting' his vehicle, so much so that he phoned me when he was diagnosed with cancer to jokingly tell me that I was going to get it sooner than I thought. My Dad bought the vehicle and gave it to my brother. He decided it was more useful for someone studying nature conservation than for a social worker to have this type of vehicle. That could have been true, but my brother was still in his first year of studies.

When we arrived at Niagara Falls, I had to use the opportunity to call my brother, as he and I have always been competitive. I found the closest public telephone and phoned him. I asked him what he could hear, and he said, "a deep booming sound." I told him it was the sound of the Niagara Falls, and that I was right there. Almost automatically, his response was "I'm looking out the window at the 4x4. I think I'm going to take it out for a drive."

Back to the UK

I returned to the UK and started working with a child protection team. This work keeps you on your toes as you have to be constantly prepared. For someone who does not like conflict, this puts you in the firing line. I was anxious about answering the phone in case I was shouted at. When I arrived back in my office from home visits, I would divide the people who had called me into two lists. Those I knew would shout at me, and those who generally did not. I would start by making my way through the list of people who would not yell at me, and when one of them unexpectedly did, and my adrenaline was pumping, I would start phoning clients from the other list. Once my adrenaline levels had dropped, I would return to the previous list.

Dad visits me in England

It was so exciting having my Dad visit while I was there. He lived in London for four years and met Mom there many years ago. He absolutely loved the history and chose to take me on an eight-hour historical walking tour. The problem with that is when it's your Dad, he can tell whether you are interested or not, so a great deal of effort had to be put into my responses, especially as the day wore on.

But we did manage to get tickets for Les Misérables. Mom always emphasised that when you go to a live show, you should sit far enough to see the actors' feet. Dad and I were highly successful in this regard as we sat on the balcony, three floors above the actors. The only problem was that we needed binoculars to spot the actors, let alone their feet.

Back in sunny South Africa

I returned home for Christmas, and with the parents I have, we had twenty-seven people over for Christmas lunch. They invited all the lonely people at church with nowhere to go for Christmas. However, work needed to be done. The warped table tennis table needed to be covered and stabilized to withstand the weight of our Christmas lunch. Hot trays needed to be borrowed, tables set, food cooked, etc. Eventually, everybody left, except for the eight people who were spending the night and the following day.

A European adventure

I was excited to visit Europe. When a friend challenged me to swim in a sea I had not swum in, as I might never get to swim in it again, I decided to swim in the Mediterranean Sea in Nice. It was January and freezing cold. It took some time, but I convinced an American girl to join me. We arrived on the beach and started removing our layers of warm clothing until we were in our swimming costumes. By this stage, the promenade was lined with spectators. We ran into the sea, submerged ourselves up to our shoulders and ran out again to the cheers of the onlookers. It was pretty darn chilly. Then, I caught the flu.

In Monte Carlo, we went to the casino to spend time with the 'rich and famous'. Of course, I kept all my money to myself and never saw anyone famous the entire evening.

Back to work again

I rejoined the same child protection team in the U.K. and loved the familiar work environment. The area office hired a car for me, and when my car arrived, I was called downstairs, given the car keys, and this gleaming silver car was pointed out to me. "It's the Escort over there." I said I did not know what an Escort looked like, but there were two silver cars parked together. He had to read out the number plate.

As soon as I put my key into the ignition, I practically had a heart attack as I heard someone talking – the radio had come on. Now, if only I could see where the lever to move my seat forward was. No such luck. I had to put my seat belt on, but I could not lean back as the seat was too far away. After about five attempts to reverse out of the parking bay, I parked nearby and returned to the office feeling slightly more confident.

After work, a colleague who also drove an Escort, explained the alarm, where to find the lights, windscreen wipers and how to open the bonnet and boot and set the radio onto the stations he thought I would enjoy. The sound system was great, although there was no CD player. If I pushed the CD button, the controls flashed; 'no disc,' yet there was no place to insert a CD until my younger brother visited from South Africa weeks later and looked under the passenger seat. Who puts a CD player there?

I am learning to manage my time better at work, which has improved my stress levels. I could never understand how my colleagues seemed to complete their work with ease, while I always had so much to do. When I questioned my manager, she said because I always smile, she figured I was coping, so she would keep giving me cases. I had to tell her that just because I smile, it did not mean I was coping. I found it particularly difficult to spend time with friends who seemed so relaxed when I constantly felt like I was carrying such a burden. I remember attending a party one night but was unable to relax and enjoy myself as I had just placed a child in foster care who begged to be returned to an abusive home rather than to stay with foster carers he did not know.

After travelling to Malaysia, Thailand, Hong Kong, China, Malaysia, Australia, Tasmania, Singapore and America; my Dad called.

My brother was ill with facial paralysis and was admitted to hospital. A few days later, my sister was also admitted. Her health deteriorated fast. No one was sure what their diagnosis was, except the medical team kept saying it appeared to be viral. Two days later, my dad called again to tell me we were losing my sister as her kidneys were failing and she was about to be placed on a ventilator to assist her breathing. I needed to get home or "You might not see your sister alive again." I stood up, told my manager what was happening and walked out of my job.

Farewell to the UK

I had been in the U.K. for almost four years. This country provided the wonderful experience of working as a social worker. I thought about staying permanently as the opportunity of earning pounds and being able to travel was alluring. If I had completed my four years, I could have applied for residency and later for a British passport. But South Africa was tugging at my heart to return, and I was ready to study play therapy.

I did not want to marry and settle in the UK, then raise my children without them getting to know their aunts, uncles, cousins and grandparents.

Before I left the UK, I told my friends jokingly that I had travelled the whole world trying to find a decent man and would return to South Africa to find myself a 'regte egte' conservative Afrikaans guy. There were jokes aplenty, and many laughs were shared after I returned to South Africa. A short while later, I met and dated Gerhardus Hendrik de Jager. What I joked about, had now become true.

A MATCH MADE IN HEAVEN

Gerhard finds his calling

Gerhard was born into a white Afrikaans-speaking family and grew up in a small rural town in South Africa. He spent much of his childhood playing with friends on the river, riding bicycles and exploring stormwater drains.

Money was tight, so they grew their own vegetables, kept chickens for eggs, had numerous fruit trees including grapevines which provided an abundant homestead. His mom never learnt to drive because everywhere they needed to get to was in close proximity, such as the school, church and the shops.

Gerhard's family helper Lina, who worked in their home, was very protective of him as they spent much time together. Before he was old enough to attend school, he would refuse to have breakfast until she arrived for work when they would sit outside in the sun while they ate together.

Gerhard struggled through school. He found it difficult to concentrate and was often distracted by his thoughts, which constantly resulted in him getting into trouble. Punishment was very different in the early 1970s, and at the age of six, he would be locked in the teacher's storeroom with the lights off as punishment for not concentrating. Of course, this did not help him focus. It made him fear teachers.

One morning, when the children needed to be in class, he was unsure which schoolbag was his as they all looked identical. He ran all the way home rather than face his teacher with his dilemma. His mom arrived with him to place a sticker on his schoolbag so he would always know which bag was his.

By the time he was in high school, he had to choose subjects based on which teachers would allow him to be in their class. He was not disruptive - he was a dreamer. Enough to frustrate a teacher to have him chased out of their class. Remarkably, he remained in school. Upon completing high school, he had already achieved the highest academic qualification in his family – but with much damage to his self-esteem.

Gerhard left school, joined the police force and placed in the Riot Unit who were used by the apartheid government to enforce peace during political unrest. Having been raised in a conservative Afrikaans family, apartheid was not seen in the same negative light as it was by the majority of South Africans.

After four years, Gerhard moved on to apprentice for the position of Fitter, working on large machines and living a very unhealthy lifestyle with excessive use of alcohol and cigarettes and very little sleep. One of his colleagues began to pray for Gerhard which he thought was quite humorous. He invited Gerhard to church one Sunday and Gerhard decided to humour him by attending. It was at this service where he felt the hand of God move and invited God into his life. Within six months, he was called away from his work into the mission field where he became a missionary in KwaZulu Natal.

He lived in a caravan and with fellow evangelists, moved a massive tent from farm to farm, where they preached the word of God and ran Bible studies. He stopped drinking and smoking.

Times were tough as there was not always enough money for food and basic necessities, yet it was during these times when he witnessed the ability of God to provide.

They would be driving along bumpy farm roads when they would notice vegetables alongside the road. Obviously, fallen off trucks whilst being transported from neighbouring farms to the nearest market centres.

Gerhard worked as a missionary for four years before being led to study theology in Johannesburg. This was a big move for a small-town young man. He left with instructions from his mom to avoid bringing home an English-speaking girlfriend.

A union ordained by God

When Gerhard and I first met, my ninety-two-year-old grandmother called us 'a match made in heaven.' People kept asking when we would get married, as there was no point in waiting since we were so well suited as a couple. Although these comments were being made, we were not dragging our feet. We met in January, started dating in May, became engaged in November, and were married the following March.

Miraculous events brought us together right from the start. I had been happily working in the UK when Gerhard prayed what I have labelled 'a lazy prayer.' He asked God to please send the right person across his path as he did not have time to look for a wife. Of course, for me, that meant packing up my life in the UK, moving back to South Africa, and finding employment in the same church where he worked. He did not even meet me halfway!

I was considering returning home from the UK in October 2001, but suddenly felt I could not wait another two months, so I moved my ticket forward by a month. Having been involved in child protection social work for four years and wanting a break from it, I asked my parents to keep their eyes open for any vacancies in churches I could apply for upon my return. Fortunately, I changed my flight. The airline was liquidated a few days after my return.

Upon arrival back in South Africa, my parents informed me of only one possible vacancy in a church, where the application closing date was 22 September. I would have missed this opportunity had I flown home in October as planned. This job was at the church where Gerhard was working, and he had just submitted his months' notice terminating his employment.

I arrived at work on my first day and met the staff who had gathered together to have mid-morning tea. Being relatively shy, I would have never walked into the staff room alone on my first day of work. Gerhard wandered past my office and invited me to accompany him to the staff room for tea. I thought this was such a lovely gesture. It made me feel braver, so I went with him. I don't know how long it would have taken me to have the courage to go on my own had I not gone with him that day.

When I arrived home later that afternoon, my Mom asked if I had met any interesting guys at work – Yes! I was getting older, and I think she was beginning to worry. I met two guys that day, but I did not realise Gerhard was also leaving so I told my Mom that I met two guys; one was leaving, and the other was Afrikaans.

One morning, I arrived at work driving my Dad's 4x4. It had a large bull bar in front, which made it challenging to navigate the space for parking between two cars in the staff parking lot. I attempted it a few times, then decided to park on the opposite side where there were no cars at all. As I walked away from the car, Gerhard called from the elevated garden of his flat and asked what I was doing on Saturday as he could give me driving lessons. I figured he did not know I was driving my Dad's car, so I shouted back that he was just jealous that he did not have a car like mine. I cringed with embarrassment immediately after I said it.

On my way to church one Sunday, I realised I was very low on petrol but decided that I did want to be late for church and since the garage was next to the church, I could probably save petrol by coasting if I needed to. So, I drove directly to church. All would have been fine if I had not left my lights on, but I did. Gerhard came over to jumpstart my car and said I should let the engine run for a while. The car then coughed and spluttered. He looked at me incredulously and asked if I had just run out of petrol. I told him I had. He just shook his head.

My brother was getting married in April, and I did not want to attend another wedding on my own. My parents suggested that if I could find someone on short notice, willing to fly to the Cape with me to the wedding of someone they had never met, they would pay for the cost of half the ticket. By this stage, Gerhard was no longer working at the church, but I did have his number. I decided I had nothing to lose and would phone him and invite him to accompany me to the wedding. I felt he was non-threatening and would not assume that I liked him as he had many female friends. I phoned him, and he said he would check his diary, then call me back. Having been married to him for twenty-one years, I now know he does not have a diary, nor has he ever had one. I did not know that then. I waited for two hours, after which I figured he was not interested. Then he called. He said he would be free and would love to join me. Since he was studying, I asked him how he would finance the air ticket. His response was that God would provide. I told him I agreed God provides, but not to attend the wedding of someone you had never met.

He disagreed. Then one evening, whilst he was volunteering at an Alpha evangelistic group course, I was with friends waiting for him at his home. He arrived with an envelope of cash, with the exact amount required to purchase the air ticket. Someone gave him the money as a thank-you gift for the time he volunteered. They had no idea of the air ticket that had to be purchased.

Later that month, we travelled to the Cape for the wedding, where he met my entire family in one evening. My parents, siblings, granny, aunts, uncles, cousins, nephews - everyone. Surprisingly, he was not intimidated. I am not one for dancing 'los' (loose), as we call it in Afrikaans. I like to dance with a partner, which I learned to do at the Afrikaans university I attended. This was an English wedding, so I did not enjoy the dancing. Gerhard asked me if I wanted to dance, and I said no thank you. I did not see anything wrong with this as there was no contract in place such as if you attend the wedding with me, I will dance with you. He was invited to the wedding and said yes. I was given the option to dance, and I said no. That seemed perfectly ethical to me.

Upon returning from the wedding, I noticed that I liked Gerhard but was not ready to make him aware of it just yet. I remember him visiting me at the office the same morning my sister visited. She jumped up and gave him a big hug. I stayed on my side of the desk and greeted him warmly. I had often joked about how the Jane Austen movie; Sense and Sensibility had two sisters whose personalities perfectly matched my sister and me.

When Gerhard left, my sister was confused about my reserved greeting of him. I responded with the dialogue from a movie my English sensibilities related to – "I esteem him greatly."

As I became more familiar with him, opening up and being more emotional about my feelings became easier. However, he still tells people he had to buy his first kiss. The truth is, he told me that if I closed my eyes, he could kiss me without me feeling it and that if I felt it, he would give me some Taiwanese dollars a friend had given him. I was adamant that I would feel the kiss, but he told me I would not, so I closed my eyes. He kissed me and I felt it. He smiled and gave me the coins. Can you believe it?

Gerhard and I get married

Gerhard was gentle and caring, and our relationship blossomed. When we became engaged, my Mom excitedly told the family. Many of them asked; "You mean Karen?" My younger sister had been dating for years and I had not dated at all. Mom had to constantly confirm that it was indeed Claire who had just become engaged. When she told Mabel who was on a step ladder cleaning windows outside, she was so taken aback, she lost her balance, fell, knocked her head and had to be taken to the clinic to be checked for concussion.

We were married on 23 March 2003. It was a beautiful wedding. Gerhard's aunt, the matriarch of the family informed us that there would be no dancing at our wedding since the date fell on a Sunday. Gerhard and I did not fight this, as it was accepted in our culture. As long as we were married that day, this was all that mattered to us.

Before getting married, Gerhard and I often discussed our shared love for children. One evening, I visited him and told him about a beautiful child I had met at one of the children's homes I visited. He immediately said he wondered if it was the same child he had been visiting two years ago at a different children's home he had considered fostering. Since owning property is a prerequisite, and he did not own property, he could not foster the child who was moved to a different home loosing contact with him. I told him there was no way it could be the same child as there were hundreds of children in welfare homes in Johannesburg.

While I was at work the following day, he visited the home. It was the same child. At this point, we were not married and often wondered what God's plan was for us and this little boy. Several miracles occurred soon after. A beautiful family adopted this little boy.

Once married and with our shared love for children, we were both ready to start a family. I was twenty-eight years, and

Gerhard was thirty-four. The most fantastic Christmas present would be a baby.

As the months rolled by and nothing happened, we became increasingly concerned and decided to start having tests to rule out any possible problems. We were both prodded and poked. It was miserable and scary. Then, once all the necessary tests were done, we waited for the results …

GOD'S GRACE IN SILENT DESPAIR

Infertility confirmed

Day 1: 11 December 2003

I was at work when Gerhard phoned me with the news. The unbelievable stress of waiting was now over. We are an infertile couple. A strange type of peace settled upon me. At least we now knew. Tears well up and are wiped away. There is no point in feeling sorry for myself; it won't change our reality. Life continues. God is sovereign. I needed to get home to check on Gerhard to see if he was okay. I expected us to cry together. But when I arrived home, he was distant and barely spoke. He was dealing with the pain the only way he knew - apologising for something that was not his fault. Later, we went for dinner with the family pretending everything was fine. With no knowledge of our situation or test results, a family member spoke with disdain about fertility treatments during dinner.

Day 2: 12 December 2003

We sang 'Happy Birthday' to my father-in-law and said we were fine, as we all do when someone asks how we are. We lie about how we really are, and most people only ask because it is 'the right thing to do' as opposed to really wanting to know how we are doing. Before leaving for work, a caller asked if I was pregnant yet. Two more callers asked once I was at work. People knew how much it meant for us to have children. What does a person say in our situation? "No, I am not pregnant yet, and won't ever be?" During this time, I started considering adoption. I would only be missing out on the pregnancy, and I would be saved from childbirth. But then, I will NEVER be a part of CREATING. It's so final yet hope still exists.

Understanding infertility

Infertility is complicated to comprehend when first diagnosed. It has become normalised and therefore accepted that you have children after you get married. One keeps hoping that maybe the test results are wrong or were placed with someone else's, and you aren't actually an infertile couple.

It's all part of the grieving process but knowing this does not make it any easier. I think it is also more difficult when you discover that some family members expected this due to a family history of infertility. It triggers anger. How is it that they did not bring it to my attention, even though it could directly impact my life?

Mom and I have always had a great relationship, and I reached out to her in the early days of our diagnosis. She was aware of the tests and the waiting and finally the diagnosis of infertility. She felt the pain intensely as a mother who could not remove or fix the circumstances her child had to confront. Upon hearing about our test results, Mom describes how she felt; "When Claire phoned one night to tell us that they were unable to have children, I was utterly broken. I felt as though my feet had been knocked out from under me. I was devastated and speechless. I wanted to hug her, to hold her and sit with her pain. I clung to God and lay awake that night as I wrestled with Him and this news. Restless prayers ensued, seeking options and searching for a way forward. It was like carrying a stone around in the pit of my stomach. Night and day; it was with me."

Infertility lives with you

The pain of infertility does not reduce or fade. Every pregnancy I heard about, left me feeling shattered. It was an experience I would never have, yet an experience so intricately linked to the very soul of a woman. Not that I was the least bit concerned about how any other woman might be feeling – my pain was too overwhelming, too desperate, too painful. The crushing feeling of never being able to have the experience of being pregnant was excruciating. I found myself self-medicating daily in an attempt to ease the suffering, despite me knowing that the pain and agony of infertility cannot be eased through tablets. I was desperate and tried anything written 'for pain' on the box even if only to reduce the intensity of it.

Gerhard said, "It is like walking through a pitch-black train tunnel with no light at the end and no way back." We had to keep moving forward without any sign that there would ever be light at the end of the tunnel whilst never adjusting to the dark. Adjusting to the dark would mean giving up hope that perhaps someday, I may have the miracle of pregnancy and a child.

Day 3: 13 December 2003

Morning tea, and I am asked by a cousin when we planned to start having kids. "You will have to ask Gerhard," was my response – shifting the attention. Gerhard was not in the room, so the subject was closed. I figured he would have more time to think up an answer than I did.

Later that day, friends arrived with their baby and happily placed him on Gerhard's lap. My thoughts kept revolving; We will never have a child of our own, and then what children will we have? Only God knows that. Gerhard circumvented my cousin's question about when we planned to start having children as quickly as I had. Tonight, I cried again in the bath as we spoke. Gerhard went numb again. He also mentioned speaking to his brother about our infertility. Is fertility treatment supposed to be secretive?

Day 4: 14 December 2003

We still have not spoken about it much. If I am alone, the tears well up, so I must keep busy. I feel guilty about all the people we will disappoint when we tell them the news. Yet none of them will feel what we feel. Gerhard does not want to tell our families until after Christmas as he wants to avoid ruining Christmas for them.

This morning, while talking to Gerhard, I say; "when we have kids one day," then stop. Silenced by a newfound reality that this will probably never happen. I know God is still in control and knows all things and has purpose in and through all things.

I sigh all the time now, every time the subject of infertility crosses my mind. We don't talk about it with each other, though. What is there to say?

Day 5: 15 December 2003

Today is particularly difficult. I am thinking about it constantly now. I have been lethargic all day. I just don't feel like doing anything. I am sighing, and my eyes keep welling up at inopportune moments. I asked Gerhard how he was doing and he said he was blocking it out. He has started sighing too and gets a distant look in his eyes. I wonder whether whatever children we will have, will be loved by others as much as they would have loved our biological children.

Silent grief and a glimpse of hope

We went for a second opinion on 16 December 2003. We have just been told with certainty that we would never be able to have children of our own. My mind buzzed with desperation. I visited a baby shelter the next day, which was part of my work, although I wanted to chat about adoption with the foster mom running the home. She had raised an adopted child, and I wanted to glean as much information as I could about adoption from her.

While with her, a lady phoned to say she was bringing her newborn baby to the home as she could not look after the child. She had been advised that the child would have a good chance of being adopted into a family if he was placed in this home and did not want her child to grow up in a children's home.

I phoned the next day. The baby had arrived, so I went to visit. It was a beautiful, little boy, and he was so tiny. We always said we would adopt one day, so I could not see the point of waiting now that our infertility was confirmed.

I took my husband to visit this little boy called Luke and sat with the foster mom to ask her more questions about adoption. Specifically, about Luke. But Gerhard did not sit for long. He wandered off, making me worry about what was going through his mind. Then he returned, holding Luke. Sitting next to me he said, "If we don't get safety gates up on our stairs at home, this little boy will hurt himself when he learns to walk." That was it. We knew he was ours!

Before leaving, the foster mother shared the contact details of the social worker who would enable us to begin the adoption process. Life is so interesting with all its twists and turns. While in the UK, I was working with children who needed adoptive homes. At no point had it crossed my mind that I might be in a position one day when adoption would be my only option for having children.

The adoption process

We were prompt in contacting the social worker to be assessed as possible adoptive parents. They were not particularly friendly and throughout the assessment – which was very expensive – they kept asking us if we did not want to wait for the next child while saving money for the assessment process as they had five families in Luxembourg waiting to adopt. We discovered that a South African family has the first option over a South African child for adoption. We could not wait for another child as we knew this little boy was our child. We wanted him, not the next one.

A family member who wanted to help, accessed the details of a social worker from a colleague whose friends had adopted a white child. Although she never discussed this with us, she assumed we wanted to adopt a white child. Instead of passing these details on to us, so we could decide how we wanted to proceed, she chose to phone the social worker herself to explain our situation and establish how they could help. What she had not realised, was that she had phoned the same social worker who was assisting us. We were still in the assessment process so when we arrived at our next meeting and were asked some rather tough questions, we were confused. Then it was explained to us that a family member phoned them and from the conversation, were given sufficient information to identify us as the same couple who wanted to adopt Luke. To the social workers, it seemed clear to them that we wanted a white child and not a black child.

We were taken by surprise. The point had been missed entirely. We were not looking for a black child or a white child. We wanted the little boy we met. He was the child we wanted. We spent three hours trying to convince the social workers. It was so incredibly stressful as it felt like we might lose him due to unintended consequences from a family member trying to help.

During our assessment, we had not realised that some of our family would have such a staggeringly adverse reaction to our adoption until we were almost through the process. We assumed our family would be as excited as we were. We realised this when Gerhard asked both sets of parents separately if they wanted the good or the bad news. The bad news, he told them, was that we were infertile and could not have children. But the good news was that they would be grandparents in two weeks.

When we told my parents, Mom burst into tears. I was not sure whether she was crying because of our infertility although I had already spoken to her about it – or the joy of our adoption. I think it was a combination of both.

Unfortunately, not everyone shared our excitement. As soon as it was understood that the adoption would be of a child of colour, difficulties with Gerhard's parents began to emerge. This idea was extremely foreign and entirely out of their comfort zone. All I wanted was to be loved and supported in creating our family and would not let others dictate whether we would have children or not and how we would have our children. This was our journey, and Gerhard and I agreed with the philosophy that; It takes a village to raise a child - not just their parents. It was vital that our child would grow up having good relationships with all family members.

As our assessment progressed, a family member, unaware of our infertility and adoption process, asked if we would need a pram or other baby goods, she was getting rid of. She said she was sure we would want to have children soon. I said yes, please, and asked if we could fetch it from her in the next two weeks. She was surprised since she knew I was not pregnant. We then told her we were in the process of adoption. She was thrilled for us.

It was incredible how God began to open hearts as we progressed through the assessment and needed to meet the financial costs of each session. We did not need to ask anyone for help, as each time we were required to make a payment, another donation would arrive in our bank account. People we would never have asked or expected financial assistance from were moved to assist with the adoption. People wanted to be involved. By donating financial resources, they felt they were. To us, this was another sign that God had chosen this little boy for us, as he was even financing the adoption. We managed to make it through the assessment process. Once we knew Luke would be coming home to us in the next week or two, we visited him with my sister, parents, and grandmother. It was so beautiful to see their excitement.

Mom replaying the moment for my benefit; "We all went to the Baby Sanctuary and were each given a turn to hold this precious little baby in our arms." She was not going to miss out on meeting and holding her new great-grandchild. Claire had to change his nappy – a poo nappy! There was much excitement and laughter. As we left, Gerhard placed Luke in his crib. I lingered. Tears streaming down my face as I watched Gerhard tenderly and gently say goodbye to baby Luke. It was a moment captured in silence. Our joy was immense.

Mom took several pictures and later placed them into a photo album for friends to page through at the baby shower she arranged for us. A few days later, we were told we could fetch our precious son, now six weeks old. We were beyond excited. We discussed names and felt Joshua was a beautiful name and that he would lead people across the racial and cultural divide as people would grow to know and love him.

We arrived at the baby shelter on a Friday afternoon in rush-hour traffic, bundled him into his car seat and strapped him in into his car chair facing the wrong way. The foster carers told us he drank a bottle every four hours. It would have been helpful if we had asked when his last bottle was.

On the way home, Josh began to cry for his bottle. We had bottles, formula, and bottle sterilisers nicely wrapped in their packaging at home, but nothing with us in the car. When we arrived home, welcome-home flowers and a Teddy bear were at the door, but we had to rush inside to make Josh's bottle. This involved washing the bottle, reading the instructions on the bottle steriliser, sterilising the bottle, boiling the water, cooling the water, making the milk – all before Josh could have his first bottle with us. Our nerves! Wow! But we did it and Josh calmed down.

The joy and pain of adoption

Many people thought our adoption was way too soon. What would have been the point in waiting? We would not have had Josh. Nothing was going to change in our lives, so what would we have been waiting for? As a social worker I could of course see their concerns; I would never have given a child to a couple who had been married for nine months from two hugely different backgrounds, who had been diagnosed as infertile only a month prior, had received no counselling and would lose the support of half their family when their baby arrived home.

In addition, they would also need to deal with society's racial prejudices, whilst both parents were completing their studies.

Thankfully, we were assessed to be competent. Josh played such a pivotal role in our healing. He turned us into a Mom and Dad, which we so longed to be. Our lives would have been empty and colourless had he not been a part of it.

The first evening we spent with Josh, my parents, siblings and their spouses - everyone fell in love with him. I had lessons on bathing, washing his hair and wrapping him tightly in his blanket. We sat for hours staring at his perfection while he slept – his hands with tiny fingers, feet and toes. Everything was so perfect, yet so small. The realisation that this perfectly formed baby was ours to cherish, hold, love, and raise. What an incredible privilege.

The following morning, Gerhard phoned his family with much excitement and enthusiasm to let them know his son had come home. The most exciting news of bringing his first child home was not shared by his family. The truth of this was tough to process. Gerhard cried. He wanted to share this moment with his family. We knew it was the start of a challenging walk. We were aware that how we chose to handle it, would define the type of relationship we would have in the future with objecting family members who were equally important to us.

It broke our hearts to realise that an innocent baby who brought so much joy into our lives, could also be seen as the reason for rifts amongst adults. Rifts others chose to create which he played no part in, other than being born with a darker skin colour. We began to believe that God would do important work in this child's life and that there would be healing and reconciliation through him. He was the most gorgeous little boy and continues to be such an incredible blessing in our lives.

To add to this pain, others judged us on our decisions and withdrew from us due to their pain of our infertility. We tried hard to repair relationships, which sometimes made me furious. We were dealing with our infertility and trying to help others cope with it and our subsequent decisions. I wanted to give up and cut out of my life anyone I felt was cruel enough to judge me. What made me even more angry was the fact that we were being judged by people who had children of their own and had no idea what we were living through.

My parents-in-law sought guidance from their ministers, perhaps seeking affirmation of their feelings. This guidance should have been objective and biblical. Unfortunately, ministers are people, with their own prejudices and perceptions. It is sometimes difficult in our human nature to provide objective clarity based on truly seeking God's guidance. Sometimes, we fall into the trap of human nature of what we think and feel. This meant that my parents-in-law received two vastly different opinions from two ministers in the same church.

During times of severe emotional stress, I found writing what I was feeling was the only way I could process and make sense of the anguish. It was also the time I allowed myself to sob.

During the initial months of feeling 'lonely' and 'abandoned' by people in our extended family because of our decision to adopt, I felt judged and targeted, and therefore resented and rejected. I was no longer being kissed hello. They would not even hold eye contact with me. It was so painful and brutal to my soul. I just wanted to be loved and accepted – I was in enough pain.

Why are you targeting me?

The same person, but no longer good enough. I am so angry, but I always have to smile. It is all about other people, never about me. 'Have compassion for others because they are hurting.' I am hurting too, and I cannot make anybody love me who does not choose to. I am who I am.

Sometimes, the pain feels too great. What is the point of trying so hard? How do you want me to be, to make your world happy? What about my world?

Why is your pain more important than mine? What makes yours any different? Can't we agree that we both feel pain for different reasons and accept each other through our pain?

Should the burden of pain only rest on me? You have lived your life and made your choices. I should qualify for the same rights. Why do you judge my choices so harshly? I am not the same person you are, so you cannot expect my choices to be the same as yours. You deny me your love because I am different and add more pain to what I am already carrying. I can cope. I am a child of God. You won't break me that easily, and especially not without consequences. You cause so much more pain for yourself and those around you by targeting me.

I was angry! At the same time, I felt I was cracking up from the pain. The pain of our infertility was just so overwhelming. It is one thing to be judged on choices you make for different people, but here we were being judged for choices we made for ourselves, which would heal our wounds. It just did not feel like our pain was acknowledged and this made it so painful to deal with.

I spent so much time sobbing because of the intensity of the pain I was feeling. It is also the only description that fully describes what it is like to cry from the depth of your being. Sobbing felt like I was crumbling into pieces inside, and it was excruciatingly painful. The pain of infertility is not like a pain I had ever felt before or have felt since. It is a unique agony. Interestingly, while doing my master's degree, one of the chapters we had to study for medical social work was on infertility. To think that I needed to underline what feelings infertile couples might have in order to memorise them for exam purposes was just mind-blowing to me, and that was just one year before our diagnosis.

What you never study though is the fact that while somebody might be experiencing these unmanageable feelings linked to infertility, they are still expected to fulfil their roles in society. As a social worker, I was constantly bombarded by people who felt needy and wanted their needs met immediately.

I began to resent people with what I saw as their ridiculous needs that were so urgent. I was now viewing life at a different pace and with a different set of perspectives and priorities. At the same time, others were living their lives just as they always had. Some days, I would be sobbing inside yet had people demanding from me due to the type of work I was involved in. It is tough to give when you feel so completely empty inside. I would probably have coped a whole lot better if people asked how I was doing. But then people don't ask, because some silly taboo exists that says; "don't talk about infertility." It is almost as though there is an unwritten law that says, "let those who suffer with it deal with it, but don't let it overflow into our lives. It's not our problem or concern".

Josh fills our home with joy

Josh adjusted beautifully in his new home. He was such a delight, and so alert. He seemed to take notice of everything around him. As he grew, he started reaching out for our faces whenever we picked him up from his cot. He would hold our faces between both his hands, and I would feel my heart throb with love for him. He was too little to speak yet, but he was communicating such love towards us.

Josh started speaking early. One of the most beautiful memories we have was when we walked around the garden with him just eighteen months old, looking for Easter eggs. This fascinated him, and he said, "There are koklits in the hlowers" (chocolates in the flowers). Even when we arrived at church, he would immediately want to look in the garden in case there were chocolates there too.

Gerhard desperately wanted to rebuild relationships with his family and have them join us in the joy of raising Josh. I could not deny that Gerhard was the man he was because of the family that raised him. This helped me commit to rebuilding these relationships. By this time, I had received counselling to deal with the adverse reactions after the adoption and was advised to let Gerhard visit his family alone. This did not seem right to me. We were a married couple, and now a family. I was not prepared to let anyone use this as a wedge in our marriage.

The social workers advised us during our assessment that we were too entrenched in our marriage. We were not independent enough from each other. We were told this was not healthy for any marriage. Yet this was the glue that kept us together. We were best friends and chose to do things together. We were acutely aware that in our current situation, we were in it together and would need to survive it together.

As time progressed, we attempted to rebuild family relationships through familiarity. We knew familiarity would change perspectives over time, but not without patience and forgiveness. We felt it would be too difficult for them to dislike someone because of their skin colour, culture or language without ever getting to know the person they disliked. It would be the concept they would dislike.

Unfortunately, people generally do not sit down and try to identify what they are struggling with and why, so they can resolve it. They tend to make a blanket decision based on general cultural norms. Our aim was to use familiarity to assist family members in building relationships. The more familiar we become with someone, the more naturally we respond to them, and the easier it is to begin building relationships. I remember camping in Parys in winter, so that family members who chose to, could come and visit us there. We would not impose on anyone but just make ourselves available for relationships to develop. It was so cold, and the campsite was alongside the river. We had our microwave for sterilising bottles, our kettle for boiling water for Josh's milk and many blankets. Every four hours Josh would wake to be fed. While one of us fed him, the other heated a bean bag in the microwave which was placed under his blankets to keep them warm for when he was put back into his cot. It was teamwork all the way.

Will the tears ever stop?

My sorrow at the inability to carry a child is ingrained in every part of my being. It is the first thing I think about the moment I open my eyes and the last thing I think about as I fall asleep. I no longer recognise myself as 'always being so cheerful' as my parents once described me. I wish for those days again when I had no concerns, and my heart felt whole. Yet, with all this pain I am experiencing, I would never choose to change anything about my family, except for our infertility.

I adore my family, and know that without this experience, we would have never had Josh. Now that we have him, I would miraculously like us to be cured of our infertility. When I pray about our infertility, I keep hearing a subtle but firm voice saying, "You were chosen." For what Lord? To suffer all this pain? We were chosen to be Josh's parents, but we have him now. Why still infertility? I don't want to be an example to others – at the moment, I don't even care about other people who may be struggling with infertility. My pain is just too great, too real, too desperate!

I feel like I am being used. Like I am here to make other's lives easier. What about mine? There is no time. Too much to do, too many things to think about. There are no escape buttons. No time off from reality. Oops! I took too long. My own pain took my attention. Someone did not get their way. I did not jump when they asked me to. I did not have the energy. I failed them.

My punishment is meted out; I must be bombarded with criticism. I am not good enough because I made someone else wait. How dare I stop to feel? This is unacceptable behaviour as I should be serving others. My pain does not need my time. It is nobody else's problem, so why should I waste time on it? I should see the urgency of others in pain. It is expected of me. They don't need to feel my pain, because it is not as important as theirs.

I've tried to pray the pain away, be optimistic, and focus my energy on the positive in life. But, when the pain chooses to rear its head, there is nothing I can do to make it go away. I must endure it, face it head-on. I must live through it. Do it alone, then pray for healing. Healing from the wounds the pain has created. Healing from the anger. Healing from the sorrow and grief and healing from the loneliness. Healing so that I will have the ability to forgive others for their ignorance yet love them anyway.

The strength to delve into my sorrow

My body tires so quickly now. I just want to sleep all the time. At times, I feel like I could explode with pent-up emotion, and at other times, all I want to do is get under my desk and hide from the world. I don't want to be around people anymore, so I don't go out of the house often. I tend just to exist most of the time.

Days come and go. Sometimes, I feel so content and happy. Then suddenly sorrow strikes. Everything floods back. All the issues I thought have been long dealt with, keep returning. The triggers keep changing. I cannot prepare myself for them, as I never know what will trigger the sorrow. It just floods back into my life, and I need to strain to maintain my grasp on control. If I lose my control, I will crumble into a heap of senseless emotions. They are standing by, ready to take over. I must keep them at bay. I must keep my sanity. I must keep my control or else my sorrow will overwhelm me.

I know what I must do. I know that I must plunge into my sorrow and pain in order to find healing. But I don't feel ready yet. I am not yet prepared to cope with the onslaught of all my emotions. I am certainly not ready to lose the control I have been hanging onto with both hands for so long. I know that I need to endure my pain in order to find healing. But the sorrow will be too great. Too overwhelming. I don't want to sink. I can't afford to for my sake or the sake of my family. I need to keep my head up. I need to keep coping.

Sorrow is so painful. It hurts to the core of my being. It won't go anywhere if I don't deal with it. But to deal with it I would have to face it. And that I do not want to do. Facing it will make it too real. I will lose control completely, and I don't think I will ever be ready for that. If I allow my emotions to well up, they could drown me. That is just too great a risk. I am not prepared for the pain at the moment. I don't know if I ever will be. I know I need to work the sorrow out of me.

How can I maintain my control and experience my emotions? Is it possible to feel these feelings without being lost in their depths? Is it possible to feel my sorrow in part, only taking on the next when I am ready for it, whilst simultaneously maintaining control? If there is a way, that is the route I need to take. I know I need to feel. I just don't want my sorrow to crush me. I need my equilibrium. I need to be able to delve as deep as I need to and then breathe again. Too deep and I will be lost. I need help to get this balance right. I must find the strength to delve into my sorrow while maintaining control. But how?

The pain and sorrow of infertility is ongoing. It is not like losing a job where you may plunge into a depression of sorts for a few months until you are on your feet again. Infertility affects the rest of your life. It will always be with you for as long as other people fall pregnant and have children, and you don't. It is a lifetime of sorrow and grief, not just a season.

As great as my pain is, I am not alone, for He who created me is constantly by my side. He knows my pain. He knows how I am hurting. I do not understand His ways or timing, but I know He has never left my side. 'Oh God, please help me! My heart's desire is to bear children. You know that! Please help my pain diminish and grant me a pregnancy. I know I am praying for my needs to be fulfilled but I am hurting so much inside, and I know a pregnancy will make my pain go away. Help me, God!'

'I am a precious boy!'

When I grew up, my Mom always checked on us at night to see if we were still breathing. It's amazing how I did the same the moment I started parenting. I would bend over his cot to put my face close to his to hear if he was breathing. As I did this, Josh would open his eyes and stare straight at me.

Josh and I created a beautiful game we would play when we were out together. I would say, "You…" and he would respond,

"I am a precious boy!" He could be sitting in the trolley while I was shopping, or we could be walking through a mall or going for a walk together. At any stage I started the game, he would respond. My heart would feel like it was bursting with love and pride.

CHANGING PERSPECTIVES:
GOING AGAINST THE GRAIN OF TRADITION

People's reactions to cross-cultural adoption

In our home, it was safe to laugh and have fun, but when we were out, we were super alert. Ironically, when people are mean, they say things to the child, not the parents. I had to ensure I was always right beside Josh, especially as he grew and toddled around. I wanted to be close enough to hear everything others said so that I could deflect what was said if necessary.

I had nightmares about people removing Josh from our family because we were white and us having to search through masses of people to find him again.

One day, when he was cooing in his pram at a shopping mall, an older lady with a gentle smile on her face walked over to the pram to see the cooing baby. As soon as she saw him, she continued walking. If the sound of a baby stimulates joy and compassion within the depths of our soul, how can the child's skin colour nullify that emotion?

In my opinion, the only way those emotions can be switched off so quickly is if there is an underlying perspective that was taught to us as children that is greater than the current emotion. Unfortunately, this is the indoctrination of racism. It is made even worse by the fact that people show no embarrassment or shame when it is so clearly visible. It triggers in me a fear of how I will ever be able to protect my children in this world from such people.

A lady at the butchery saw Josh and Gerhard together and asked if Josh was his son. When Gerhard said yes, she made her way around the counter hugged Gerhard, and said, "Thank you!"

Different perceptions from different people. We all have a choice in life. We can choose to love, or we can choose not to. We can teach our children to love, or we can teach them not to.

I recall a young man in a restaurant where we were dining. He spoke loud for us to hear about "these white South Africans who take children away from their own cultures" and all kinds of nonsense without knowing anything about the situation at all. Had they spoken to us and not about us, we could have cleared some of their imaginings. The truth is Josh would have grown up with a family in Luxembourg had we not adopted him – very far from the culture of his birth or anyone that looked like him.

What frustrated me was people accusing us of how we had wronged a child when they would never lift a finger to help one. They were not interested in children needing their own culture, they just did not want people of colour entering their white spaces. It was heartbreaking and I ended up in counselling trying to process it and work out a strategy for responding to these kinds of comments that would be made when Josh was older and able to understand what people were saying. Racism is ugly, painful, and difficult to protect someone against, as it rears its head when you least expect it - until you begin to constantly anticipate it. Public campsites, swimming pools, restaurants and shopping malls were usually where we required constant protection against a known enemy – racism and the unknown striker who would feel the need to openly and coldly air his racist beliefs.

I recall when our family went on a camping holiday and made our way towards the heated swimming pool. Josh took the lead when a teenager heading towards the pool, walked up to him and started chatting. The teenager repeatedly commented on how well Josh spoke English. We told him twice that English is Joshua's home language and was the only language he spoke at that stage. This teenager could not overcome his surprise that Josh spoke with no accent. It is in times such as these, when we realise how entrenched we are in our perceptions.

Josh starts preschool

With Gerhard completing his studies and going out to work, Josh had to start attending preschool. When Gerhard and I first discussed it, he sat on the couch and cried saying that it begins with creche, then primary school, then high school, then university and then your child moves out of the home – he felt it was happening too quickly. I remember being surprised at Gerhard's reaction as Josh was only eighteen months old. We still had many years together with him.

The classroom assistant in his preschool loved him. I think she felt sorry for Josh because he had white parents, so she became very protective of him. She showed me how to brush his hair, what type of brush I needed, and how to moisturize his skin twice a day. I knew she loved our Josh, but I was in trouble regularly for not brushing his hair to her standard or sending him to school without moisturising his skin.

Fetching Josh from preschool was the most beautiful experience. He would see me from a distance and run towards me with his arms outstretched. I would bend to pick him up and he would hold my face with both hands. I would kiss him and hold him tight. The love I had for Josh was indescribable.

Josh loved preschool. He could not understand why his school would have holidays and would stand at the front door with his schoolbag, crying on days when there was no school.

One day, I arrived to fetch him from preschool, when a teacher told me there had been an incident between him and another child. Josh told the child she was white, which upset her as she felt he was calling her names. When it was reported to the teacher, she reassuringly told the child that indeed she was white. This upset the child further as she said the teacher was taking Josh's side.

In our family, even filling petrol could be entertaining. One day, Josh was seated in the back seat while the petrol attendant was filling the tank. He looked up, saw Josh and immediately addressed him in an African language. Josh responded loudly in gibberish. I immediately asked Josh what he was doing, thinking how rude it was of him. His response was "He did it first."

His sense of humour has never failed him. In Grade 0, I was called to the school because Josh had rung the school bell indicating the end of lunch, halfway through lunch break. This caused about sixty children to run to their classrooms with the teachers left to sort out the ensuing chaos. As the teacher said, it was funny the first time, but Josh had now repeated this exercise five times.

This little boy held my heart. He was special and so loved. But I wanted more children. I wanted siblings for him. I wanted a bigger family. I felt selfish for wanting more and not being satisfied, but I sincerely wanted more children. Gerhard and I always dreamed of having a big family. But now was not the time. Not yet.

It was vital that Josh would know about his adoption and be emotionally secure before continuing to grow our family. Thank Goodness Gerhard and I agreed to this. He was the realist when I at times would get caught up in the need to be impulsive and have another child. He would always lovingly bring me back to my senses.

People's opinions and understanding of infertility

People are infertile for several different reasons. However, it always amazed me how people who did not know the details of our infertility would comment about how they were infertile, yet still had children. Hence, it's a possibility for everyone. I wished people would not talk from a place of minimal understanding to make us feel better. The ignorance of these comments fuelled my anger.

For someone who barely experienced anger before infertility, I felt I was angry so much of the time. Angry that people were ignorant and would create so much pain. It amazed me that people would talk rather than listen. I realised how opinionated people are and how they use their opinions to feel good about themselves by thinking they were actually helping, rather than establishing where you are, how you are doing and attempt to meet your needs.

Maybe I spent too much time thinking because of my situation where others just seemed to react. I had to keep reminding myself that in my mental state, I was much more sensitive to what people were saying and doing than normal.

Interestingly, some of the more painful opinions were from pregnant women who were excitedly awaiting the birth of their children, yet so harsh in terms of telling me to move on. They seemed to have all the solutions for what I needed to do and should do based on my circumstances. I wanted to scream and point out the injustice of our circumstances. I knew this would not solve anything or change their opinions. I had to accept that they would never fully grasp my pain or my thoughts because where I was, they could never be.

It's another day, and the pain starts afresh. A phone call — "I have a baby for you." My emotions start racing…It is too soon, but can we turn down a gift of this enormity? Will we ever receive such an offer again? The inner turmoil; the questions, timing, finances, coping skills. Would we manage two young kids so close in age?

I was talking excitedly to everyone. What other news could make my life so emotionally turbulent? I know Gerhard is not ready. I know Josh is still too young. But I am being offered a baby. A miracle I cannot have myself … and I have to turn it down? Even though I know it is the correct decision to make, it is so difficult. It makes my heart weep. Then our friends give birth to the miracle of their own son the next day. A few days too early. I have not prepared myself adequately yet. Help! I'm crying inside. Yet, I want to be excited for them. The spear has shot deep into my heart again. I cry out in pain, but no one hears. It's my own pain. My own darkness. My own, from the depths of my aching soul.

Why do others say so much without thinking? Do I talk like that too about things I know nothing about? A pregnant lady wants to know why I would be interested in a baby that has not yet been born. After all, there are so many abandoned babies needing homes. I have tried many different places. I cannot afford a child that has already been born which is why I am thinking about this child. This opportunity. This miraculous offer. I'm thinking; You will give birth to a newborn child. I will never have that opportunity. Due to my unfortunate predicament, I must not want a newborn child. I must take an older child who has already been waiting for a home.

How is it that you can have what you want, but I cannot? We are women with the same needs. Why must I take on the guilt of society to ease people's burdens? If you have such a heart for abandoned children, why don't you do something about it?

My children are still a private decision between my husband and I. We do not need to know what you think or feel. You can decide to have your children at any time. We cannot. We have to depend on another women carrying a child for nine months in her womb, then maybe, if we are lucky, for her to decide to give that child to us. We will take any miraculously created child we can. If the child is a newborn, what a bonus! We will do what is right for us.

We are tired of pompous pregnant women and pompous Christians; "If you pray harder, God might hear your prayers." God does hear my prayers. He hears the groaning from deep within my soul. He also has plans that we do not always know about.

Why not try to be supportive and love us as before? Before we became second-rate citizens to you? Please! No more "If I can have children, then anyone can". Rid yourself of your pride and feel with us for a while? If the truth be known, you don't really care. Your concern is shallow and self - centred.

Since we still don't talk much about our pain, I ask Gerhard to write about how he is feeling.

Can it be nauseating?
Infertility, I mean.
Yes, it can.
It is the first thought that comes to mind when I think of it.
Nausea!
Eating away...
at my stomach lining
my thought processes
my religion
Yes! My faith!

Can I avoid
 pregnant women
 tiny babies
 young toddlers
teens?

They're everywhere!
Constantly reminding me of it.

It is so easy for you to say, "Go for fertility treatment!"
Do you know what you are saying? You speak like an imbecile.
Like a bull in a China shop.
That is what you are.
I don't need plasters or superficial solutions to hide the infection or treat the surface.

I feel cursed! Yes, I know what the Bible says.
I feel cursed. No, I don't want to talk about it.

Have you read the book by So and So?
You know, So and So who could not have children?
They went to Dr. So and So, and now they have three kids.
Did they test you for...?

Have you heard of...?
Yes, yes!
I have been there and tried that.
I'm not a specimen – a guinea pig.

Have you seen the movie "Maybe Baby?"
Yes, it's funny.
Real life is not.
Neither is handing over the sample bottle to the receptionist.
I fail to see the humour in it!

Criticism has risen to destructive levels in our lives. It feels like a tidal wave is bombarding us. If we do not hang onto each other as a couple, we will be torn apart by this great force.

Time to leave

Why had we not thought of this before? It made so much sense. We could move to the UK, where I already had four years' work experience and be free from the family pressures that were tearing us apart; the opinions, advice, judgement and criticism. We could leave it all behind and learn to laugh again. This seemed like the perfect solution. The decision was made. We both applied.

We felt it necessary to meet with a Christian counsellor and pastor who had also been Gerhard's mentor for many years to discuss our plans. He was also the special man who married us. A few days after we met, we received a letter from him.

Here is a copy of his letter dated 31 January 2005.

Dear Gerhard and Claire,

It was good meeting you both recently and hearing your thoughts on a possible move to the UK. I wondered if it would be helpful for me to give you some feedback on my thoughts after our session.

I've heard you both speak more than once of your desire to return to the enjoyment of one another and friendship you've enjoyed more fully in your relationship in the past. I realise that your friendship with one another is very important to you both, and I'm grateful that your relationship and communication with one another matters to you as much as it does - this is your best gift to Josh, your love for one another.

I was aware that much of the focus of our session was on the pros and cons of going to England. I am very open to your going, and I respect the fact that in the end, only you can discern God's leadership in this.

In light of your desire to grow your relationship with one another, I'd rather ask; "What will it take for you each to learn how to better communicate what is going on in the depths of your hearts to one another? How can you ensure that the pressures fallen upon you are not as a result, in part, due to you being closed off from one another?" I wonder if these seem significant issues to you.

I believe you both have all the potential for a deep and valuable marriage which can sustain you and your children, and people who come into your home far into the future.

My prayer for you is not so much about where you find yourselves living in the future, but much more for you both to grow in understanding yourselves - individually, and also in learning increasing intimacy by letting one another into your respective worlds – a scary thing for all of us.

I have high regard and love for you both, and you continue to be in my prayers.

With love to you both,
Vic.

We are going to the UK – Well, No, actually!

I attended social work interviews in three cities and received three employment offers. Each one was a two-year contract where they would fly us over and organise our visas. My previous work experience in the UK was a massive advantage. What fascinated me in the interviews, were the questions about my willingness to work with people from different ethnic and racial backgrounds. They appeared content with my response that we were a cross-cultural, trans-racial family that was English, Afrikaans, Black, and White.

Having decided to emigrate to the UK, we experienced the most incredible change. It was as though the family withdrew all their opinions and pressure, previously placed on us. Suddenly, we were left with extraordinary support. No one telling us what to do. Just people loving us. It was so reassuring and refreshing, it made us wonder what support we might experience in the UK on our own. It left us reassessing where we felt God wanted us to be. Suddenly, moving to the UK did not feel like the right option anymore. This was confirmed when Gerhard's employment opportunities did not materialise.

From left to right: Grandpa Tom, Claire, Gerhard, Granny Marion
Front from left to right: Mikey, Katie and Josh

Joshua, Mikey and Katie

Gerhard and Claire

Josh and Claire

Gerhard, Claire, Oupa, Ouma, Mikey and Josh after his Dedication

Claire, Gerhard, Josh, Mikey fetching Katie the day she came home

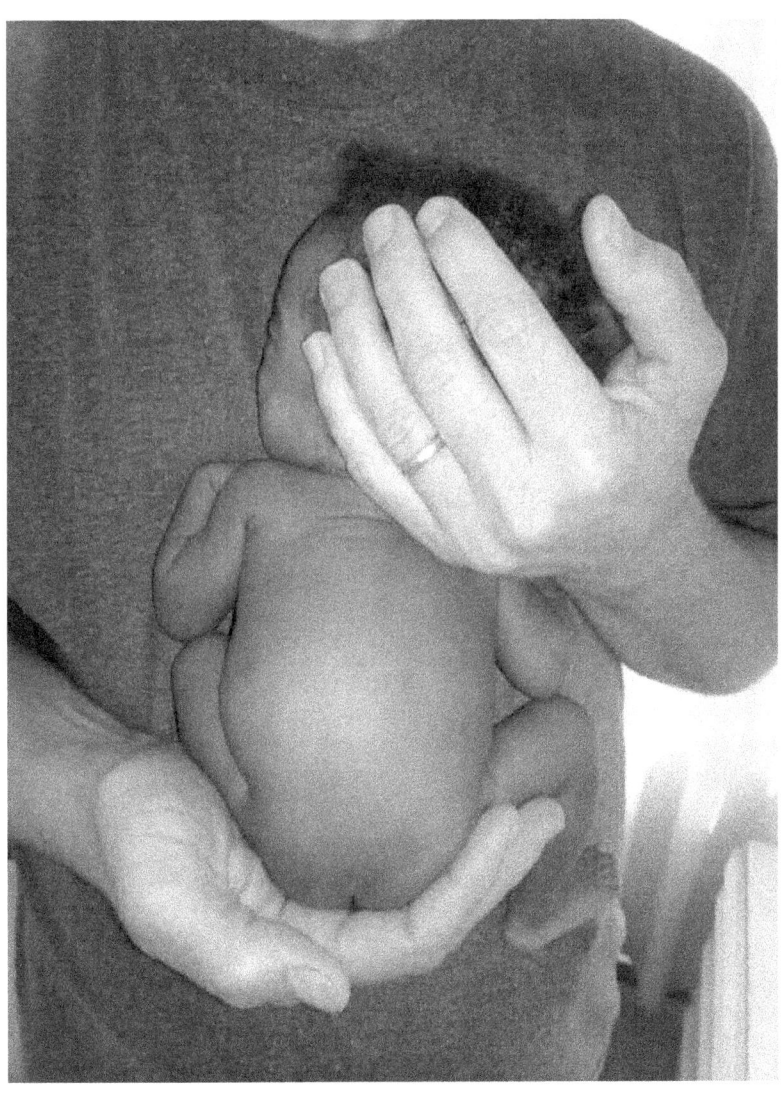

Katie being held by her dad

Katie and Mikey

Josh on his eighteenth birthday with Grandpa Tom and Granny Marion

The wondrous joy of adoption

Josh is getting so big now. He is adorable. I will forever be grateful to the lady who carried and gave birth to him – our unique, precious son. God is so good that even in the midst of our turmoil and pain he has blessed us with the greatest gift – a miracle of life. His timing is perfect, too. Josh helped us to keep our sanity. With all the pain, sorrow and grief we are experiencing around our infertility, God has blessed us with a son whose daily antics keep us smiling and remembering that life is hard, but God is good.

I made a point of cuddling Josh after his bath, in his bath towel in front of the mirror every night. It occurred to me that if Josh always had white people around him, he could one day have a sudden revelation that he is black and looks different to us. I did not want that to ever happen so I thought if we chatted, laughed, and hugged, while seeing ourselves in the mirror, he would grow up seeing and recognising our differences and accept them as being normal rather than having a shock revelation. I wanted this little boy to see and know that he was loved deeply for precisely who he was.

Our housing complex had a phone connected to the security guard at the entrance gate. The guard would phone us before granting permission for visitors to enter. Sometimes Gerhard would pick up the phone and say 'guard, guard' to attract his attention and inform him we were expecting a visitor. We never thought much about it until Josh stood on his little chair one day, grabbed the phone and started shouting "God! God!" He had been observing Gerhard and thought he could speak to God through the phone.

On another occasion, Josh walked into the lounge where Gerhard and I were sitting and said, "I have a message from God." We were dumbstruck. Why would God send a message through our two-year-old instead of talking directly to us? We told Josh we were listening and asked him what the message was. He just kept repeating the same sentence, leaving us confused. Then he toddled into his room and came out with the storybook 'Jonah and the Whale,' and turned to a page with the picture of Jonah being thrown overboard where he shouted out, "I have a message from God." I read that story to Josh often, so you would think I would have remembered that sentence. It showed how attentive Josh was during his nightly bedtime stories. He enjoyed nighttime storytelling right up until he was fourteen years old, but never developed the love for reading himself.

Mornings were special, and Gerhard would sing out; "Josh!" and Josh would sing back from his cot;" Daddy!" It was so beautiful to hear. They would do it so naturally. This would be repeated about three times before Gerhard, or I would fetch him from his cot and bring him to our room. Josh knew we would fetch him, so there was no urgency as he and Gerhard played this game. It became our special ritual every morning.

We attended an Easter egg hunt at church. There were marshmallow easter eggs all over the garden. If you found a coloured piece of paper, you could exchange it for a giant bunny Easter egg. Josh found a piece of paper and received his giant bunny Easter egg. On our way home, we were approaching a red robot when we noticed a little boy standing on the side of the road with his mom begging. Josh asked if he could give the little boy an Easter egg. I told him they were his, so he was welcome to. Since he had about twenty marshmallow Easter eggs, I expected him to give one of these Easter eggs away. Instead, he took the giant bunny Easter egg and handed it out the window to the little boy without a second thought.

THE WAR WITHIN

The War Within

I visit a friend who says she has never wanted children and thinks she might be too selfish to be a mother. I mention how I would love to conceive, yet it remains a dream beyond my reach. She suggests I consider the possibility that maybe God did not think I was ready to be a mom yet. What! Josh is nearly a year already. I AM a mom. God has proven his belief in my capabilities by entrusting the life of a beautiful child who grew in the womb of another. I am HIS mother, and he is my son.

It made me wonder whether in her opinion, motherhood was limited to being pregnant and carrying your child yourself. What a misconception! Motherhood starts with giving yourself to a child in every way; including being there for the good and the bad, loving like you have never loved before, hurting with them as you have never hurt before - including moulding and guiding them. In many respects, motherhood requires giving up your life to invest in the life of a child who is exploring and experiencing their world whilst trying to make sense of it. What a privilege! The notion that adoption does not turn any woman into a mother when you take on the responsibility for the gift of another's life is ignorance.

And yet, often I felt I was a second-rate mom. Never fully qualifying as a mother because I did not have a birth story. It did not help when people in my life suddenly felt compelled to consistently tell me exactly how they thought I should be caring for and mothering Josh. I sensed people somehow felt it was pregnancy that prepared you for motherhood. That it was pregnancy that enabled you to know how to look after a baby from birth, but for an adoptive mother, you needed help. Unfortunately, I reached a stage where I could not brush aside these comments. I started feeling angry about being made to feel like a second-rate mom when I knew I was a good mother.

Once again, I turned to writing in my journal to channel my anger.

Second-rate mom?

Am I a second-rate mom? What makes me know less than a mother who has carried her child in her womb? A biological mother knows no more about raising children than an adoptive mother. Pregnancy is not a form of enlightenment. The hormones don't suddenly play a role in teaching parenting skills. So why do you feel you know so much more than me? What makes you think your experiences are superior to mine?

God created us differently including the experiences we would encounter. Why don't you attempt to learn from my experiences instead of constantly trying to 'stuff your suggestions down my throat?' I am so tired of your continuous barrage behind my back about what I am not doing, that I should be doing. Of course, I should be doing it only because it is the way you do it. We have come to learn that according to you, only your way is right.

Why so narrow-minded? Do you feel you are better than me because I have never carried my own child? Do you realise the pain it causes me each time I feel you are looking at me like a second-rate mom? Don't I deserve some respect? Why is it always about you, and never me? I want to be a good mom to my child, but I also want to feel like a good mom. I adore my son and will always have his best interests at heart, even if he did not grow in my womb.

In the same way God blessed you with children, he has blessed me with a child. I don't think it serves any value as to who carried my child or gave birth to him. The gift is my child, and I will always strive to be the best mom I can. Save your critical thoughts and judgemental attitude. They are of no value to me. I need to believe in myself so my son will learn to believe in me and himself. Your method of breaking me down and making me feel like a second-rate mom because you love my son is nonsense. If you love my son as much as you declare, try building me up and loving me unconditionally without constant criticism. That would be a gift. One my son will directly benefit from. The continual criticism places me on guard. On defence. Of course, I am not strong enough to fight back when I am criticised or bullied into a corner. So, I end up feeling angry and bitter towards myself because of all the things I would have loved to have said and how I should have responded. But you heard none of it because none of it was said out loud. Why should only your voice be heard? Aren't you interested in what I am thinking or feeling? You say you love me, but I don't see it.

I am a good mom. Over time, I will learn to be a better mom. I will learn from those who have the time to invest in my life – those who love, care and mentor me. God blessed me with a child because He knows I am a good mom even if you don't think so.

I decided to take some time out to attend a retreat run by our church. I felt it would be a good way to draw close to God again.

The journey into myself

28 January 2005

I am sitting at a retreat at St Benedict's in the south of Johannesburg. I have just discovered one of the areas of real struggle for me is not the issue of infertility itself, but the way in which others view me because of our infertility. When we first adopted Josh, I did not feel I qualified to attend mother and baby groups as I had not experienced giving birth to a child and, therefore, was not a mother in the true sense of the word.

I do feel like a mom now because I am doing mom things. And yet, I have such a sense of other mothers 'looking down' on me in judgment as though I am not a real mother. I know that I struggle with how I think other women see me and not how they actually see me. I need to focus on my identity – who I am in God, not who I am in the eyes of other women. I need to stop judging myself.

29 January 2005

Today, we studied Ephesians 4:1-16: 'I urge you, then – I who am a prisoner because I serve the Lord: live a life that measures up to the standard God set when He called you. Be always humble, gentle, and patient. Show your love by being tolerant with one another' – Good News Bible (1982:241)

This reading reminded me that I must not settle for second best. I must live a life that measures up to the standard God set for me when He called me. I constantly compare myself to others instead of to God. I fear confrontation and am very self-critical about 'cheating' my way into motherhood – telling myself how others perceive me. I need to remember; it is God's standard I need to measure up to and not the standard of the world. I also need to learn to speak the truth in a spirit of love with humility, gentleness, and patience.

Wow! I sure need to learn more about tolerance. Although I feel entitled to be intolerant toward critical and ignorant people I dislike, I know I am no more entitled to intolerance than anyone else.

What really amazed me about this Scripture verse is that it took me back to 1999 in Malaysia where I as a single twenty-five-year-old, was sitting with a friend I had just met. She asked if I would mind if her friend could speak to me.

I was a little surprised but said it was fine. Her friend arrived a little later, clutching a brown paper bag containing a Bible. She took me aside and asked if she could pray with me. She then told me she had been given a prophecy for my life. She read me this verse saying that I must live a life that measures up to the standard God set for me when He called me. She then added that God had said I should not be concerned about a life partner, finances or about children.

I thought this was all so strange as I was single and happily travelling the world earning pounds with no concerns about having children. None of these three things were of concern to me then. What I did not realise was that God was already preparing me. I was living in my 'seven fat' years and He knew my years of 'famine' would descend upon me whether I was prepared for them or not.

God was offering me comfort before I knew I needed it. He was preparing me for what was to come, ensuring that when I looked back from these challenging years, I would never be able to say He left my side. He was with me in my darkest places before I arrived at them. What an awesome God we serve!

The day's session continued:

What do I need to overcome to be fully me?

The points I was looking at were:

- I need to overcome resistance within myself. (This meant; feeling I am not good enough, or second-rate)
- I need to overcome the resistance I feel from others. (This meant; feeling judged and criticised)
- I need to overcome the resistance I have towards the task itself. (This meant; how do I plan to tackle the problem at hand? Infertility – How do I plan to live through it?)

In this session, we learnt that only through God can we fully recognise our true self and our potential within ourselves. We need to dismantle our false motivation of self, which drives us but is not true, and hinders us from growing. Our false motivation comes from a sense of false self we have built around ourselves. That part of us in constant monologue with ourselves, overcompensating and fearful. Needing to be in charge of what we do for God and comparing ourselves to others.

I think my biggest challenge is resistance from myself as I keep telling myself what others are thinking of me and my circumstances. I tend to listen far too much to my voice. I believe God will show me the way through a difficult and daunting task. I need to be quiet before God in order to hear His affirmation. This is essential if I am ever going to feel on par with mothers who have given birth. Not spending time seeking God's affirmation is why I feel the way I do about being a second-rate mother.

I must realise that even in pain, I am part of a bigger picture. I need to rest in the peace of knowing that God will guide me. I do not need to perform, just to surrender. I have significance because God values and guides me. I do not need to worry about what others feel about me because I know I am of value to God, the Creator of the Universe. This journey of learning to trust God will take a lifetime, but it is the road to freedom. I need to overcome the resistance within myself to ensure that I am walking this path. It is the only path leading me out of my pain.

Whose voice do I listen to? Who has the ultimate say in my calling to Christ? Who must I be submissive to? Who has control of my life? My resistance is the struggle to let go of the control I want to have over my own life, which includes the ability to have children naturally and when I want to. If my life is surrendered to Christ, I can no longer be in control of it. I must have faith in my calling and my ability to fulfil God's calling in my life. And one of my callings is to be a great mom to Josh. If God had called me to this task as He has, He has given me the ability to fulfil it. What great news. If God can believe in me, it does not matter what anyone else thinks. What freedom!

What is my calling?

I need to be a vessel through which God's light can shine. I need to be full of God's colour and life. I must have optimism and humour for God to restore me to wholeness—even in my infertility. Playfulness is essential as it celebrates life. I must remain focused on God and seek His direction alone for my life without worrying about what others might think or say.

I need to stop looking at the millions of directions others are pulling me in as they pull me back and slow me down from ultimately reaching the goal God has set for me. If we had discussed Josh's adoption with the family, we would have been so slowed down in the process, that we might never have had him. Instead, we knew he was our gift from God, and we remained steadfast and focused as we moved towards our goal of his adoption, informing the family of our decision only once it had been made.

Today, I learned that healing my infertility can only happen through God – not through others. My call is to keep my eyes on God, my Guide. He has the whole picture. He knows his plan for my life, and He is the only One who can show me the way. Thanks be to God for His glory, wisdom, and grace when we make mistakes.

Although I learned a great deal today, I was left with a struggle. I have missed Gerhard and Josh so terribly that I can feel the physical pangs in my stomach. If I had a car at the retreat, I would have returned home yesterday evening. Yet, I am on a retreat to meet with God. I should be placing God first. My focus here should be on God. Is it sinful to be so attached to my family? How do I focus on God and place Him first when my love for my family is so intense? What needs to be changed and how do I change it?

30 January 2005

What shift has God brought about in me this weekend? I have learnt that I seek affirmation from people and not from God and judge myself by people's standards and not by God's standards. I have felt God walk with me along the path as I walked in the garden – to feel His presence so close was amazing. I have learnt that He does not sit in heaven and direct us but walks beside us step by step.

I have just realised what a big part fear plays in my life – fear of losing someone I love. That's one of the reasons I have pined so much for my family while I have been on this retreat. It feels that if I am with them then they will be okay. I have to hand their protection over to the Lord. I can't protect them. I need to entrust them to the Lord. Why do I struggle so much with entrusting them to the Lord? Do I struggle to trust Him?

Who am I?

Buried feelings

Sometimes, the feelings are buried so deeply that I can't seem to find them. I am ready now. I know I need to face my pain. It comes welling up when I am not looking for it, and now, when I want to face it head-on, I can't find it. Where does it go to hide? Where must I go to find it? Why does it run when I am now prepared to face it? I must delve deep within myself to see and draw it out. But I don't know how. I am ready to face it now. I am prepared to feel it. I know I need to spend time with what I feel. I can't just push through without feeling. If I do, my feelings will just stay buried until next time.

Who am I? Can I risk the adventure and pain of getting to know myself better and growing in myself? I need to go through the process of getting to know myself better if I am going to find where my pain goes to hide. I also need to be willing to let God in and to allow Him to change me. I need to remember that within God's love, I can risk knowing myself better and growing in maturity, wisdom and stature (Jeremiah 31:1-3). What changes do I want to see in myself so that I don't end up wasting my life?

- I need to let go of my need for control.
- I need to trust God with my life.
- I need to believe that God has my best interests at heart.
- I need to rest assured in Christ's love for me.
- I need to leave others' opinions out of my sphere of concern, remaining focused on my Father and His guidance for my life.

I am struggling!

Two special people in my life are now pregnant. I am really struggling. I have received beautiful, personal, exuberant phone calls announcing their pregnancies twice. The pain is unbearable. I desperately want to be excited for them both, but I am fighting with my own emptiness.

One of them goes for their first scan. They are ecstatic. They phone us from the hospital to ask if they could come to show us the scan. Of course, we agree. I put down the phone, and we both hold back our tears. How are we going to manage this visit? The intensity of their excitement is the intensity of our pain. We are both silent – suspended in our own world of despair.

They arrive. They are bubbling over with excitement. We muster the courage to ask the questions we should. We are so happy for them, but so intensely sad for us. Then they take out the scan to show us. I am dreading this moment. It's easier to adjust to someone being pregnant when we cannot see any change in them, but the scan will be so much more challenging to digest. It will make the pregnancy so real, and I don't know if I can cope with that.

They show us the scan. There it is – that tiny dot. The miracle of a life beginning. It's such a tiny dot of hope. A dot we cannot have. I am ready to burst and explode with pain. It feels like I am being ripped apart. I ask her what it feels like. Joyful enthusiasm is bubbling out of her. Usually, it is contagious. Not now. Not in this context. Not when I am in this much pain.

My feelings are so ambiguous. This is my best friend! I want to be thrilled for her. I hate the way my pain is in the way of celebrating with them, but I cannot manage it. It is too overwhelming. We both try to get excited for them, but our pain shows through. Thank goodness it does not dull their enthusiasm.

After they leave, there is silence. We both busy ourselves around the house. I wash dishes. Later, we chat. Our experience of seeing the scan was so similar. How could such a tiny dot make our hearts sink? We both know that the dot has all that it needs to develop into a healthy child. That dot is a child that is just not visibly recognisable at present but will be a fully developed child in nine months. What a thrilling miracle – but not ours!

I wonder how I am going to get through my life without ever falling pregnant. Will I survive? Will my marriage survive? I so want to be carefree again. I used to be so happy. I want to feel like that again. Will I ever feel like that again? Will the intensity of these feelings ever fade? Will I ever be able to get on with my life as a normal adult? I just want this pain to stop.

Is the miracle beyond my reach?

The miracle I want to be a part of is beyond my reach – the miracle of carrying a child within me. It is a dream that most girls have, and my dream has been shattered. But I am in it now. I need my pain to be understood for what it is. This battle that is constantly raging within my being is so difficult.

There is not much written on infertility. Who can help with the intensity of my feelings? How can I express them without creating pain for my family? And yet, I need an outlet, and I need it now. I have to be heard. I can't cope with this struggle on my own. It has been trapped inside for too long. I need to talk about it now. I need to breathe again. I need to face my pain so that I can move forward. At the moment I live by the rhyme: 'Pain, pain, go away. Come again another day.' When will I get to share it? When will I be in a position to deal with it? When will the pain go away? When, when, when?

A LEAP OF FAITH

Thinking about fertility treatment

- The idea is not attractive, but we could have a child born to us.

- The risks would be great – what would we tell our children if it were successful?

- What would our families say, or think? Why should we care or feel guilty – they have never been in our situation.

- If God intended for us not to have children, then how is adoption acceptable, and why would He have given us Josh?

- If our infertility is merely 'nature's default,' would God be happy for us to attempt other routes of our choice?

- Would having children through fertility treatment be a purely selfish means of fulfilling our needs? What about children paying for the 'sins of the father?' Would we be creating children just to bring destruction upon them?

- Could we keep fertility treatment a secret for the rest of our lives? No. Would we want to? No. So then what?

- Am I sick for even thinking along these lines? Would I be dropping my 'standards', or have I always been judgmental?

How many other couples choose this route? Why does it feel like we wouldn't? Can it really be so bad?

How is it that people who had our backs and supported our adoption, don't support us in having infertility treatment? So, they are not supporting us as a couple as we struggle to create our family, but instead, they support what they believe is right for them. But this is us and our family. What happened to love and support? Why has judgment replaced it? We continually feel judged while still trying to manage our emotions around infertility. It's sad how people can love you when you do what they believe is correct yet are unable to support you as you wrestle with what you believe will be right for you.

Guilty, guilty, guilty!

I am always made to feel guilty. Guilty about my feelings. Guilty about the only options I have available. Guilty about how my options make others feel. Guilty about how I should feel. Guilty that I feel anything at all. Carrying the guilt everyone places in my path. Everybody has an opinion. I have to constantly defend myself in order to survive. I feel guilty about how I make everyone else feel. Others are annoyed that my pain should enter their domain. Why should they have to deal with it? It is my problem anyway. I feel guilty that my pain affects their lives – nothing like being the topic of conversation.

Everyone knows how I should solve my problem, although none of them have experienced it. Advice emanates from every corner. Everyone has a solution – except me. No one else has to live with the outcome – except me. So why so much advice? Will it stop the cycle of pain for others? Must I feel guilty because I am now thinking of myself? My life. Amazingly, I have one too. Or at least I had one. That was when I was in control. But control is slipping, sliding away from me. My grasp has weakened. Is there any help now? Where do I go from here? Who can change the course of my life if I lose control? No one. I must fight to get control back and hang onto it with all my might.

Let's go for treatment!

I lie in the bath, which is my favourite place to relax. It's the end of a busy day and Josh is asleep in bed. My husband walks into the bathroom and says, "I think we must go for fertility treatment." My mind is in a spin. What? Where did that come from? Gerhard has always been so opposed to fertility treatment. It seems he has done a great deal of thinking to arrive at such a decisive statement.

Panic fills me. I don't know if I am ready. Yet, hope begins to infiltrate this hopeless situation. What if I had the treatment, and it worked? I could be pregnant! We agreed to schedule an appointment with an infertility specialist to have some of our questions answered. Once we decided, my hope began to rise and filled me with a sense of cautious excitement like I had not felt since I cannot remember. The 'What ifs…' began flooding my mind.

Our journey into fertility treatment

As Claire's Mom, I prayed unceasingly for a way forward for Claire and Gerhard. One day, Gerhard visited our home to work on his laptop. He sat at the kitchen table while I was busy at the stove. My heart was aching for them as we chatted. Suddenly, Gerhard walked over to the sink and turned to face me. With that, he slowly slid to the floor, saying, "We have decided to go ahead to seek Infertility treatment." I slowly dropped to the floor joining him as the immensity of what I was hearing began to filter through my aching. I felt the presence of God envelop us, and the realisation that we were standing on holy ground. Genesis chapter 3 verse 5 and Joshua chapter 5 verse 15 flooded my mind. We sat in stunned silence. I wanted to take my sandals off. I cried. We hugged. I praised our Almighty God. It was a revelation. God had it all together. A moment I will never forget and remains indelibly imprinted in my mind.

Our journey into fertility treatment started. We made an appointment and visited the clinic. We were assessed, blood was taken, and the process forward discussed. Fairly soon thereafter, the injections started. I received daily injections into my tummy, further injections at the clinic, and more blood tests. Our hope was alive. This was it! I was going to fall pregnant and have the experience I had so dreamed of.

Fertility treatment fails

Treatment 1: Failed! Thyroid not functioning!

Treatment 2: Failed! Progesterone levels too low!

Treatment 3: Failed! Even with medication to increase progesterone levels!

Treatment 4: Failed! Possibility of poor eggs

Treatment 5: Failed! With injections to improve the quality of eggs and medication to increase progesterone levels.

The fertility treatment failed again. That is five failed treatments. We agreed to do only five treatments, so that's it for us. No pregnancy. No carrying a child inside of me. What we discovered is that I have hormonal issues that affect the success of fertility treatment. What we once saw as a 'quick fix' situation, we see as impossible.

When dreams die

The pain pierces so deeply, it feels it will never stop. It feels physical so I take painkillers to help dull it. Will it ever go away? We prayed and prayed for our fertility treatment to work and for us to be blessed with the miracle of watching a child grow inside me, and our prayer was unanswered. I know God hears us as he has answered many of our other prayers. Why? What are we supposed to be learning from this experience? Are we just such slow learners? Is this why the treatment fails time and time again? What if we are experiencing this pain in order to help others one day? Why on earth would anyone want to endure this pain in order to help others?

At this point in my life, I don't care about others' problems. Why is God not hearing our prayers? Then to hear on the day our final treatment tests are negative, that God has given an already completed family an unplanned pregnancy. What? Did He make a mistake? We were praying for a child, and He gave them another one. Where is the sense in that? Why? Why another one for them? Why not just one pregnancy for us?

I know God does not make mistakes, but my heart is yelling "Hey God! You've made a mistake, we're over here? Why not us God?" He could change everything in a second, and I could become pregnant. But he has not done that. I am confused because I know

God will give me my heart's desire. This is it. Has God not seen how badly I want to carry a child? Is it still not obvious enough? What else must I do? The rebellion inside me wells up.

I know God is righteous and I know He has plans for my life. But I want a pregnancy, and I want one now. I want to be in control of this area of my life. I want the freedom to choose how many children I want to have and the size of the age gaps between them. Just about every woman gets this privilege. I want it to. It is my right. I want this more than anything in the world right now, and there is not a darn thing I can do to get it. I am helpless.

I am so numb; I almost feel relieved the trauma of the treatment is over for good – so are my chances of ever carrying a child. My dream is lost. It has died and so has a part of me with my dream.

Adoption is the only other option we have - we will have more children. This decision will have repercussions on our extended family. We need to prepare our families. But how? I decide to write a letter…

Our family,

I needed to take the time to write to you to give you a little insight into where Gerhard and I are at the moment and how we are doing.

As you are aware, we all get to a stage where we desperately want to have our own children. Gerhard and I are no different. The struggles we have faced have at times felt insurmountable. Our smiles often camouflage the pain and sorrow we have felt and continue to feel as it cuts so profoundly through us. Our struggle to have children has not yet come to an end. We both desperately still want another child. Our struggle will continue until we too can bask in the joy of our children. Unfortunately, we will never experience the joy of the miracle of a child growing in me or watching my tummy when the first kicks are felt. We will have to allow another woman to experience that joy with our child as we did with Josh.

Life is a series of choices. In the current circumstances, The only option available is for us to adopt again. You, too, are in a position to make choices. You can love and support us in this challenging time or decide not to. You are entitled to make your choice.

As a couple who loves and respects our family, we pray deeply that you would choose to embrace our special family as it grows under the guiding hand of God. We also pray for our future children and their safe journey into this world. We ask that you join us in this prayer.

May God bless you richly.

A perfect letter, I thought. Straight to the point. My decision was made, and I really did not care what other people's opinions were. I was fed up that with everything we did, others felt they could judge us. I wanted to once and for all state where we stood and let people know that I would live my life and make my choices. I was no longer going to worry about others and suffer guilt for the pain I was causing them. I experienced enough pain of my own. This was my life, and I was going to live it. I felt the letter expressed precisely how I felt. So did Gerhard, but He would not let me send it.

Have you ever noticed when you have a fertility problem, the whole world feels they are invited into your marriage to join you in making decisions about how you will have children? If you don't have fertility problems, having children is a very private thing between you and your husband, and no one interferes. Interesting, isn't It?

Confusion and a solution

So! The treatment has not worked. I'm not pregnant. I now feel ready to adopt. I want a baby! We have now been through five treatments and realise fertility treatment are as addictive as gambling. It is so easy to just try again because 'maybe this time...' I could not do this to myself now. I could see myself starting to gain some control over my life again. I could visit children's homes, contact our social worker and feel like I had a definite chance of having the second child I so desperately wanted. Going for treatment again would just delay things more and Josh was almost three years old already. I was so worn out emotionally, I believed no matter what treatment I was given, I would never fall pregnant in this state.

I contacted a children's home and put my name down for a baby girl. They did not currently have a baby girl available, but said they would contact me as soon as they did. At least I felt like I was going somewhere.

I get a phone call from a friend who is involved in counselling a young pregnant mom who plans to give her baby up for adoption. The baby is due in about two weeks. The mom is unsure of the sex of her baby. Am I interested? Yes, of course!

The young mom has her baby, and it is placed safely in care. I let my husband know the baby has been born, as I wanted to contact the social workers. He just shakes his head. He needs a six-month break. I want to know whether the baby is a boy or a girl. He says he does not think knowing would be a good idea. I am feeling frustrated and desperate. I am so ready for another baby now. I have already waited so long with so many disappointments. I have this gnawing feeling. There is a tiny baby lying in a cot, desperately needing a mom and dad. Here we are with an empty bedroom. Parents desperately wanting a baby. Why are we waiting?

One last time

Then our fertility specialist phones and asks to see me the following day. I go in to see him. "Let's do one more treatment and change it slightly. Maybe it will work this time," he says. I knew I could not. I arrive home and discuss this with Gerhard.

He convinces me there would be no harm in trying one last time, adding the re-assurance of never to try again if it did not work with the changed treatment.

My mind is closed. It has failed five times already. Why would it be any different this time? My mind tells me to just get on with it and adopt. I figure we should adopt, and if the treatment works, great! If it does not, we still have our new addition to the family. The pressure will be off as we will already have a son and a daughter. Gerhards request for a six-month breather before we adopt is still in place. We move forward with the treatment.

The doctor assured us the injections they use would ensure my emotional state would not have any effect on my hormones. In fact, they would be entirely controlling my hormones through the injections. That gives me a flicker of hope – not much, but a flicker is good.

Treatment starts next month. Meanwhile, Josh is approaching his third birthday. The age gap between him and a sibling is widening, and I'm still struggling through the same issues. Although I would love the experience of pregnancy, I believe it would be in Josh's best interests to have a sibling who looks like him. If we adopt now, we will meet his needs in terms of age gap and a sibling who looks like him. Then, we can still attempt the treatment. But I have agreed that if Gerhard needs a six-month break, then that is what we need to do.

We go through the two weeks of heavy treatment we now know so well, then wait expectantly, for two weeks. I continuously tell myself that if it did not work this time, we would not lose anything. You can't lose something you've never had. What mind games I have learnt to play with myself – but they never really helped when the treatment failed as each time my heart felt shattered into millions of pieces.

We go through the waiting period and then have the blood test. By this stage, I refuse to ever have a home pregnancy test again. I had only ever seen negative results which meant I would end up going for blood tests anyway, since the home test was not always accurate. Nowadays, I go straight for the blood test. It is accurate and there is no false hope. Now, we wait for the results of the blood test.

Success at last!

Oh, what glorious news! We are pregnant! God has created a life in me. In me! My God has given me my heart's deepest desire. I now carry a life within me.

My Mom described her experience of the day we found out we were pregnant: 'One day, they came down our driveway, leapt out of their car, and came running to our house, calling out, 'We are pregnant! Mom and Dad! We are pregnant!' A momentous moment! Such excitement! And gratitude, joy, tears, blessing, and giving God the glory.

Many people ask why I am making it public knowledge so early in my pregnancy. Very simple. I have never been pregnant before. My pregnancy is a miracle on its own. I have no idea whether I will be able to maintain this pregnancy or not. For now, I am pregnant. I might not be by next week. The world must know I am pregnant so that if I lose this child, they will know I was once pregnant. So many people have been praying for this miracle in our life. They deserve to know that God has answered their pleading – even if only for a time.

I am not focusing on my baby yet. I don't want to hope too much. I have already been through so much pain. I am on hormone treatment to help maintain the pregnancy and I will take one day at a time. I am pregnant at last!

Four months into my pregnancy I receive a phone call from the social worker at the children's home. They have a baby girl who is a few weeks old. My heart immediately felt we should take her. Why not! She needed a home; we needed children. The age gap between the baby I carried and this baby at the home would be sufficient. My husband did not share this thought.

God blessed me with a husband who is sometimes less spontaneous than I am. Looking back, he was right. I was so tempted at the time to go and meet this little girl just to see who she was and to hear her story. But I knew better. There would have been no way I could have walked away after I had met her.

As my pregnancy began to show, Josh's excitement increased. He was so excited to be getting a sibling. I remember him sitting in the back seat of the car one afternoon and asking me if his baby brother would look like him. He never mentioned colour, and I could not assume that was what he was asking. I learnt always to answer questions excluding the colour component. If it was explicitly raised, I would answer that question. I responded that Mikey would be a boy and have a winky just like him, which seemed to satisfy his question.

We had a later incident at school when I arrived a little early to fetch Josh, and all the children were still at the table finishing their lunch. As I waited for him, one of his classmates confirmed that I was Josh's mom, but I did not look like him. Thankfully, I knew her mom who had brown hair, and this little girl was blonde. I spoke to her about how people in families don't all look the same and asked if she looked the same as her mother to which she said no. We chatted about people having different colour eyes, hair, etc. She and the other children seemed quite happy with the explanation and moved on to discussing other things. It was essential for me when these conversations occurred, Josh would not be made to feel different. That they would recognise how everyone is different and unique due to various characteristics.

THE WONDER THAT IS OUR BOYS

A new identity – again?

Once pregnant, you are no longer an 'infertile.' You are experiencing something infertile couples long for. You realise your success in falling pregnant has placed you into a different category – that of 'being normal, like everyone else' and yet you still have that bond with those left behind in their struggle for pregnancy. You can feel their pain because their pain was your pain. It does not just vanish because you are pregnant; your struggle has shaped your identity.

I often feel the pain even though I have children as it is usually triggered by someone else's struggle or a flashback of my own experience. My struggle remains so much of who I am. I will never know life without this struggle. My family was designed and created by God around this struggle.

Probably the most challenging aspect of adjustment for me was when I, overcome with excitement about our miraculous pregnancy, began to share it with others and received responses like "I thought you said you could never have children?" It felt like I was being accused of lying now that I was pregnant, rather than people celebrating this miracle with me.

The two options left available to me were either to divulge every detail of my fertility treatment to prove that I'm not a liar and never was, or to keep silent and be left with anger and hurt welling up inside due to the person's ignorance. This, just when things were getting better!

The grief of infertility is so personal, as is the celebration of a miracle pregnancy. For someone who has not experienced infertility, endured infertility treatment or walked the painful road with someone who has, they will never understand that miracles happen where possibility does not exist. Infertility is in no way black and white.

Mikey is born

The pregnancy went so smoothly after the difficulty of falling pregnant. All went well, and we booked an expected delivery at the hospital in advance. At 39 weeks, on my sister's birthday, I discovered I was bleeding heavily. I screamed to Gerhard in panic. We piled into the car and raced off to the hospital. All I could think of was God could not let me lose my baby now – not after all we have been through.

We rushed into the ward, and immediately, the staff connected monitors to my tummy to check my baby's heartbeat. The nurse said it did not sound right, but I should not stress because my baby could just be sleeping. I was so stressed; all I could think of was that I was about to lose my baby. The gynaecologist arrived, and the theatre was booked for an emergency caesarean.

The nurses' concern subsided as the monitor appeared to register that Mikey had been sleeping. Still, the gynaecologist was increasingly concerned as he felt the bleeding was because of the placenta rupturing. He would not be able to determine whether it was continuing to rupture or not until he operated. If it continued to rupture, Mikey would be left without oxygen.

I was rushed through to the theatre. Three needle attempts later, and the epidural began to work. I asked the gynaecologist how long it would take to get my baby out. He said 7-10 minutes. I knew if my placenta had fully ruptured, my baby would not stand a chance. It would be too long for him to be without oxygen. It felt like ages, and then the gynaecologist lifted out a beautiful, healthy, screaming little boy. He was alive and fine. What a relief! My placenta had only partially ruptured and so had continued to sustain Mikey. Thank you, God!

Loving brothers

Josh was so excited to meet his little brother, he wanted to hold him. We sat him on the empty hospital bed next to me whilst he rocked Mikey singing 'Baa, baa, black sheep.'

The love for his little brother extended to our home after Mikey and I returned from hospital. He was so incredibly protective of Mikey. One afternoon, I put Mikey into a camp cot for his nap. Josh spread a blanket on the carpet next to the cot as he said someone had to stay with his brother to keep him safe while he slept.

Often at night, when Mikey would wake to be fed, Josh would wander from his room to lie with us, quietly chatting with me or falling asleep. In the day, he would sit next to Mikey to eat and kiss Mikey all the way up and down his arms. Seeing the love these two brothers had for each other was beautiful.

Being the youngest, Mikey had the smaller of the two rooms, but Josh insisted that we had to move his bed into Mikey's room so that he could keep him safe at night. At almost four years old, Josh was super responsible. When we realised Josh intended to share the room with Mikey long-term, we moved them both into the larger room.

By this stage, Mikey was old enough to move into a bed, so we had a bunk bed for the boys. Mikey struggled to fall asleep at night, unlike Josh who fell asleep easily. He would watch all the antics from the top bunk as we tried to get Mikey to sleep. I would rock him, pat, hum and sing to him. Eventually, he would fall asleep.

Whilst Mikey enjoyed being sung to sleep, Josh loved stories and chatting. He always chose whether he wanted a story or a chat. We quickly learnt what an incredibly social child Josh was. If he was naughty and was sent to his room, he would be out within minutes with a changed attitude. Mikey would spend hours in his room playing and exploring with his toys and was quite happy to stay there rather than coming out to apologise.

When Doctors diagnosed Mikey as needing grommets, we took him through to the hospital for a day procedure to have them put in. After Mikey woke from the anaesthetic, he started crying inconsolably. I held him, Gerhard held him, Granny held him, but he just kept crying. A hospital cleaner walked into the room, and Mikey immediately stretched his arms towards her. This kind-hearted lady immediately put down what she was holding and took Mikey in her arms. He immediately calmed down. As he was too young to express himself in words, we assumed he wanted our helper, Regina, and just felt completely comfortable with this lady who reminded him of her.

A busy bundle of energy – that's Mikey

Mikey was busy even before he was born. He kicked so violently from inside that I was nervous his foot would come right through my tummy at some point.

From the moment he started balancing on his feet, he would run everywhere. Ideas would shoot into his head and needed to be actioned with immediate effect. The speed at which he moved was terrifying – especially as a mother trying to keep him safe. Up until age three, I would have to strap him into his pram and walk down the very middle of the aisle whilst shopping to ensure he could not grab anything off the shelves.

To every person passing us, he would shout "Help me, I is stuck, I is stuck!" I cut all sugar from his diet in attempt to calm him. Once, I had a mom passing me in a shop saying, "Sugar high, hey!" No! This was Mikey without sugar. By four years old, we had progressed to restraining his movements with a material band attached to his wrist, and the other to mine. Mikey hated it. We reached an agreement where if he remained in the shopping trolley, we did not have to use any further restraint, but the moment he climbed out, he would have to have this band attached because he was a runner of note.

Mikey loves machines

Mikey loved water and machines from a very young age. He received mops for Christmas three years in a row. While watching movies at home, Mikey had a rolled-up extension cord he used to place next to himself to stroke.

He did not sleep with a teddy bear but with the 'ironess.' This was an iron one used to press clothes. Thankfully, he started with a little plastic one he would take wherever we went. Soon he had outgrown his plastic 'ironess' and wanted one made of metal. Gerhard had to take the plug off an old iron for Mikey to play with. One weekend when we went to stay with Ouma, we discovered we had forgotten it. Gerhard had to take the plug off an old iron for Mikey to use for comfort in his bed as he went to sleep that night.

Lawnmowers were Mikey's other big fascination. He loved them and decided anyone with a lawnmower was his friend. He would be so upset with us if whilst driving, he would see his 'friends' on the side of the road cutting grass with lawnmowers and we would not stop for him to talk to them. We had to ask the security guards in our complex to ensure Mikey did not sneak out on the trailer of the garden services.

Mikey inherited a pair of gum boots that were about two sizes too big for him, but these became his 'worker man' boots. He wore them everywhere in case he needed to work. He 'helped' the gardeners, he 'helped' the guys laying fibre for the internet, he 'helped' dig and fill in trenches, anything that kept him busy physically.

Josh deals with primary school

Josh's enjoyment of pre-school lasted until Grade 0. At this stage, he could not understand why school moved from 'just playing' to 'doing stationary.' He would wake me early every morning to remind me he did not want to do stationary, a term he used for schoolwork.

We discovered Josh was a remarkable athlete and was selected to run in the South African Christian Schools Sports Association (ACSSA) championships in Durban. During one of the years Josh was chosen to participate, we were on a very restricted budget. Whilst driving to Durban, Gerhard said the petrol gauge looked as though it was broken, since it had barely moved. It turned out to be the hand of God providing for us. Not only was it not broken, but we arrived in Durban on one tank of petrol and drove around for two days until we needed to fill up, just after Gerhard's salary was paid. It was one of those miracles people could not believe, but it happened to us.

At one stage, we were told we needed to buy Josh a pair of spikes for athletics. We priced them, but due to cash flow difficulties, we were unable to purchase them that week. That evening, Gerhard arrived home from work and told me he had been gifted some money. He wanted to know if we should spoil the children, by buying them take-outs, until I explained that it was the exact amount of money we needed for Josh's spikes. When Gerhard walked into Josh's room and said, "I heard you need to get spikes," Josh immediately jumped off his bed and said excitedly, "Did God give us the money?" I absolutely love that our children recognise that provision comes from God and that God holds each of us in the palm of his hand.

The complication for Josh in primary school was that when people knew he had a white family or a white sibling, he was always asked questions. Josh's reaction to this was evident when we went shopping; he would always walk a couple of steps behind us pointing out how others observed our family when walking together. He was convinced of his observation where no one paid attention when he walked a few steps behind. Whilst no one was being rude, they were interested. However, Josh was not keen on drawing attention to himself and possibly being asked questions. We have encountered our fair share of adults who openly ask inappropriate questions in front of our children, indicating extraordinarily little thought or compassion before and during speaking.

For about two years, Josh requested that Mikey not mention they were brothers when they played together at a campsite or where people did not know them. Mikey found this particularly difficult as he was proud of his older brother and would often say 'my brother' before realising it. Immediately, children would be fascinated and ask Josh questions. This triggered sibling conflict with Mikey as he tried to understand why Josh did not want anyone to know he was his brother.

Mikey's funny antics

Mikey's busyness was such that he was often in trouble. While tucking him into bed one night, he said, "I is a naughty boy!" It broke my heart as he was consistently in trouble. That day, he turned on a tap at pre-school which activated the playground sprinklers, wetting most of sixty children. He did turn on the tap, but he had no idea it worked the sprinklers.

After this incident, we banned the word naughty from our home and changed our wording when he was in trouble to "I cannot believe such a good boy would make such a bad choice!" It worked, after some time. I did not want him feeling he had to live up to the 'naughty' title.

Mikey would climb the burglar bars whilst his teacher required the children to sit quietly on the carpet. He needed to move constantly. One afternoon I arrived at school to fetch him whilst the kids were playing with wooden blocks. As I looked towards the group of children, I suddenly heard a child cry. The next moment, Mikey broke out of the crowd of children, ran across the playground and placed himself in timeout. He was only two years old then. He had thrown a block that hit a little girl, so he knew he was in trouble and would be sent to timeout, so he just took himself there.

I arrived home from work one day to have a computer mouse presented to me. The cable had been cut about 15cm from the mouse itself. With so much pride in his voice, he said, "Look, Mom, I cut it all by myself!" He had destroyed the mouse and was proud of himself. I did not know how to react. Should I share his excitement at his ability to cut it by himself or show my disapproval for something he has now destroyed? What kind of child proudly displays his destructive behaviour to his mom?

I remember conversing with my Dad about how busy Mikey was and how I was anxiously waiting for him to reach the age of five without him breaking any bones. My Dad thought I should prepare myself for an older Mikey who would most likely participate in high adrenaline sports like jumping off waterfalls. He thought I should consider the likelihood of Mikey being at the forefront of this type of sporting activity. We had to cover this young man in prayer!

One night, Mikey suddenly asked me to 'lullaby' him and then hummed so I would understand what he wanted. That started me lullabying to him every night until he was about eleven. To my surprise, he asked me to lullaby in his bungalow at a cub camp. I wondered whether it would embarrass him as I did not have a singing voice. He told me it would help all the other boys, too. I asked permission from the other boys, and they joined me singing as Mikey drifted off to sleep.

Mikey was not too keen on swimming lessons. The teacher struggled to get him to straighten his knees, so during one lesson, she placed Mikey on the side of the pool and asked him to walk like a robot. He looked confused, so she exited the pool and walked around it with straight arms and legs, not bending her knees or elbows, to show him how straight he needed to keep his knees while swimming. She then repeated this exercise during the following lesson.

Josh was sitting with us during this lesson. When the teacher again emphasised to Mikey that he should straighten his knees, Josh told her that she did not speak Mikey's language. She looked perplexed, pointed at Mikey's knees, and asked him, "What are these?" He responded, "elbows," so she had to ask him to please kick with his elbows straight.

Mikey stood in the pool area with his Dad one morning and called, "Hey Dad, look here!" Gerhard had just worked on the Kreepy Krauley pool cleaner and placed it back into the water before looking up. He immediately realised Mikey was underwater. Mikey battled so much with the water that he fought his way to the surface so Gerhard could grab him. He could not swim yet emerged with the biggest smile. He pin-dropped so silently into the water that Gerhard did not hear him submerge himself. Mikey was genuinely impulsive and fearless.

Mikey really take things literally

Mikey was incredibly literal in following instructions. When giving him instructions, we had to ensure he understood them as we did and not add his own interpretation.

With Mikey being so literal and specific, one of Josh's biggest teases was to say to Mikey, "I'm black, and you are white." It drove Mikey insane. He would be annoyed responding, "Your hair is black, your skin is not black. I have brown crayons, and your skin is the same colour, and I am not white. You are brown, and I am peach." Josh loved getting Mikey all worked up around this, laughing as he stood his ground. "No, I'm black. Do you have a problem with it?" "No, you are brown, and I am peach!" Thankfully, they both grew past this teasing.

Sometimes, we also have to be careful about being too literal. One day, Josh asked if he was brown around his mouth, pointing around his mouth with his finger. My instant response would have been to say yes, but I had learnt to clarify what was being asked rather than just assuming. When I asked him what he meant, he spun Mikey around and repeated, "Am I brown around here like Mikey?" They both had been eating chocolate. Mikey had it smudged all around his mouth, and Josh had no chocolate around his mouth. That was the question Josh asked – not was his skin colour brown, but did he have brown chocolate around his mouth?

Bright Mikey has dyslexia

Mikey is very bright, but as he grew, we noticed certain struggles within the classroom setting. Learning letters was just about impossible. Counting was a battle. He could not understand why we all had to count to ten in the teacher's way and why he could not count to ten using all the numbers in the order he chose. Doing homework would mean getting him to practice counting to ten in the teacher's way, after which we would allow him to count to ten in his way. By the end of Grade 0, we had to move him to a smaller school, and after the first term of Grade 1, we moved him to a remedial school.

Diagnosed with severe dyslexia and dyscalculia, we started him in extra lessons, remedial classes, speech and occupational therapy. He was thrilled if he could repair something that would help someone. He once brought the faulty paper shredder home from the psychologist assessing him and repaired it for her.

Slowly, this busy boy who was so full of life became ever so quiet as I dropped him off and fetched him from school. Once home, he would disappear into the garden to design the latest irrigation system he spent the day thinking about. This would revitalise him until bedtime, when the tummy aches would start and continue through into the morning with tears and him rolling around on the ground. He never fought getting into the car to go to school. He obediently got in and just went silent. We decided this was destroying him and took him out of school. He response was "I told you God did not make me a schoolboy!"

Mikey said that when the teacher tells him something, he forgets it the minute she is finished talking, but when he watches something, he remembers it because it keeps replaying over and over in his mind. We turned to video-based homeschooling. For the first time since attending school, I realised Mikey had an innate ability to remember facts. His learning was phenomenal in every aspect, so we engaged Maths and English tutors to provide lessons since he struggled with these subjects.

During his homeschooling years, Mikey would accompany his granny shopping so he could calculate the cost of everything she bought. However, she would keep losing him every time he saw someone with tools. One example was of a guy with a drill. On another occasion, it was a ladder.

Mikey has the gift of helpfulness and is sufficiently intuitive to anticipate when help is needed before anyone realised it. Once whilst with his Dad who was repairing something, realised his Dad would need a specific tool and proceeded to fetch it. On his return, he presented it to his Dad. He was always one step ahead with his intuition and knowledge of tools.

Later, we moved him back to a physical school where he could enjoy the social aspect of learning while being tutored in the way he learned; mixing his grade subjects and obtaining higher grades in the subjects he could manage, and lower grades in the subjects he found challenging.

I'm back again!

What incredible healing God has set in action in my life. I still experience being run down and stressed more quickly than before infertility issues ever arose. It is as if my coping skills vanished with the intensity of the sorrow I experienced.

I wished people might recognise some of my old self in me. My pre-infertility days. That someone would mention I look happy or even cheerful. That would be a gift to me, rather than the immediate concern for my well-being when any type of normal stress occurred. On Thursday 12 June 2008, it happened. I arrived at my son's school to fetch him, and on our way out, one of the teachers looked at me and said, "You are always so cheerful when you come in here – it is so refreshing."

She had no idea of the longing I had to hear those words. I have been so broken inside, and God has been rebuilding one block at a time for so long. My healing is taking place and is visible to others. It is visible to the outside world. God has been refining me through this tormenting fire and is gracious enough to allow me to remain me – changed, yet better. He never intended to allow me to be broken beyond recognition, just to be moulded and shaped as was needed for His Kingdom's purpose. What an amazing God we serve!

Our family now

We are now the proud parents of Josh and Mikey. What a joy to be parents. Not without hard work, I must add. We have battled our way into parenthood and bear the battle scars. These scars whilst hidden, exist deep within both of us. We have found healing through our children.

Josh, now seven, is a gentle, quiet character. I call him my 'cuddle-bug' as he thrives on being hugged and cuddled. He loves just to be loved. He is a deep thinker who asks questions beyond his years, often leading us to expect more from him than should be expected from his age. We make mistakes as parents but pick ourselves up and try again.

He loves being around people, and although apprehensive when meeting new people, he blossoms once he gets to know them. He has also developed a wonderful, playful sense of humour and loves to trick people or play jokes on them. He is our tender-hearted child. His heart is big enough to fit the world into it and has the most compassionate spirit towards children. He will protect anyone he feels might be vulnerable due to their size or disability and will happily entertain babies and toddlers for hours on end.

Mikey is three and is bright and busy. He learnt to run at ten months and only slowed down to a walk at two and a half years when he started to talk. He loves music and is very playful and without fear of older children. He is our 'go get 'em' child who always takes the lead. When questioned about initiating mishaps, admits it was him with a huge grin across his face. No fear, just pride at his accomplishments!

Two completely different children. Two separate miracles from God entrusted to us by our Creator. He trusted us with their lives. What an incredible privilege and responsibility our children are.

JOY COMPLETE

Infertility is a lifetime companion

The pain does not end here. It is a lifetime companion. It does not disappear because you have children. The pain is substantially reduced, but in a moment, without warning, when I hear of someone else's struggle or someone else's pregnancy, I can still be brought back to that place of excruciating pain and the tears flow again.

Mostly, other women's pregnancies have been less painful and more exciting for me since I have had my own. People's struggles and desperation to have children still engage with my soul on a level that I cannot build walls against for protection. I am not sure if the pain will always be there but for now, it is.

Sometimes, I feel like my need to have another child is like an addiction – I have this desperate need to have more and more children. I suppose it's linked to knowing the impossibility of it, and now having found a treatment that has brought pregnancy into the realm of possibility for me, it makes me feel like I do not want to waste time. Unfortunately, there is a disconnect between this intense need and our finances.

A year on …

The feeling that our family is not yet complete and that we need a little girl has been eating away at me, becoming quite overwhelming. Gerhard feels it, too. We have often chatted about it openly, so the boys are aware of how we feel. Josh made this clear while chatting to his Ouma on the phone about Mikey having just learnt to swim. "Mikey knows how to swim now Ouma. It's only my little sister who does not know how to swim, but we don't have her yet!"

A return to fertility treatments

With much prayer and discussion, Gerhard and I made the decision to return for fertility treatment with the hope of a third child, possibly a daughter. The idea was exciting and seemed quite simple. We would just have the same medical intervention that worked when we had Mikey. There should not be any issues. Alas! It was not to be that simple again.

Treatment 1: Failed

Treatment 2: Failed

On the Tuesday night after our second fertility treatment failed, I was absolutely devastated and phoned my Mom in tears. I felt we were throwing our money away and that adoption made the most sense as we would be guaranteed a child. I spent the night sobbing and wondering what plan God had in store for us. I felt so defeated, again. But, as always, God had a plan, and we had to trust in His perfect timing. He had to ensure that we were prepared and ready for the plan he had in store for us. The truth is that the fertility treatment had to fail. How could God give me a pregnancy when he had created my little girl, and she had already been born?

The next morning, I received a phone call from a friend who was a social worker. She had no idea we had just had a failed fertility treatment and told me she was at a children's home seeing a client and had just seen their newest baby. The little girl was premature, and they wanted to place her in a home as soon as possible. She said, "Your name keeps coming to mind. I am not sure if it is God or just me, but I thought I should phone and let you know."

I immediately phoned Gerhard to tell him I thought we had just found our baby girl and described the conversation I had with my friend. We needed to meet with the social workers to clarify a few things, like whether the mom used drugs during pregnancy, etc. Gerhards response was clear and direct; "There is a little girl who needs a mom and a dad, and we are a mom and dad that needs a little girl."

I managed to contact the social worker on Thursday, and she arranged to meet with us the following Monday morning. We arrived with all the paperwork they requested. We chatted a while before they brought the tiniest baby girl for us to hold. They then asked if we would like to proceed with the process. Imagine a baby awake and looking directly into your eyes. What could make us want to pause or stop the process?

The assessments went on into the next week with home visits, police checks, meetings with the boys and chatting with them about having a little sister. We were told we could fetch our little girl on Thursday. This was in two days. The excitement in our home was tangible. My sister upon hearing our news, went straight onto Facebook to request donations. In three days, we had everything we needed: clothes, cot, pram, bath, nappies, bottles - Everything! Josh was only eight years old, but he helped his Dad put the cot together for his new sister.

Premature Katie enters our lives

Thursday arrived, and we chose to keep both boys home from school so that they could come with us to fetch their little sister. It was important to us that the boys could meet their little sister before the rest of the family arrived at our home to meet her. Four-year-old Mikey walked into the children's home carrying the car seat. He immediately recognised the social worker who had spoken to him, and with absolute confidence, he placed the car chair on the ground, pointed at it and blurted out, 'My sister needs to go in here so that she doesn't get hurt!'

Katie was brought to us in the home waiting area, and the boys were fascinated by how tiny she was. She was born three months premature at 1.08kg and weighed 1.9kg. She was a little niggly and we were told that she was due a feed. Immediately, both boys sat down, asking if they could feed their baby sister. The compassion towards Katie from her two brothers who had only just met her was contagious; their excited chatter, their concentration as they fed her, the gentleness they showed her. It was so precious.

When Katie had been fed and we were getting ready to leave, we were introduced to the crisis pregnancy counsellor. This special lady had walked a path with Katie's biological mother and had visited Katie in ICU for six weeks while she was there, twice a day, in order to feed her milk with a teaspoon as her sucking reflex hadn't developed yet. What a privilege it was to meet someone who had played such a pivotal role in our little girl's life.

We gently placed Katie in her car chair and climbed into the car with the boys, telling her that we were going home and explaining what our house looked like. I'm not sure that Katie was listening though as she slept the whole way home.

Shortly after arriving home, Granny, Grandpa, and her aunt came excited to meet her. Granny just sobbed with joy when she saw Katie. Katie sat on her grandpa's lap, and they stared deeply into each other's eyes. She was home! We had our little girl, and she was so loved already!

We met with an adoption social worker the following week to finalise the legalities. We knew we had to pay fifty per cent of the process upfront and needed more available cash. God's grace and provision were poured out on us once again. We received a phone call from the minister of the church I had grown up in. He said an envelope had been dropped off at the office and asked if we could collect it. Upon collecting the envelope, we discovered that it was filled with cash – the exact amount that we needed for the initial payment for the social worker! We have no idea who dropped off the envelope, but only God can provide that type of help. We now had the money to move forward with the adoption process, which included further social work assessments, court reports, and magistrates.

The home that Katie had been at had a particular parenting programme that was compulsory for all prospective adoptive parents to attend. Due to Kate being premature and needing to be placed with a family as quickly as possible, this happened before we participated in the parenting programme. They asked us to commit to this programme, which we did. Things were therefore a little 'backwards' this time around in comparison to the adoptive process we had followed for Josh. This is just indicative again of how every child is different, so each adoption is unique in its own way.

When Katie arrived home, I was afraid to bathe her because she was so tiny. Gerhard bathed her in the beginning because I was just too nervous. He had such big hands compared to this tiny little girl, but he was incredibly gentle with her. He was a doting daddy from day one.

It was fascinating that all the organs needed for a human being to function were inside this tiny little body. Everything necessary for this little girl to grow into an adult was in place. Each organ so tiny yet functioning perfectly. How incredibly miraculous!

Different colours

Being the oldest, Josh has always been in Mikey's life since he was born. So, for Mikey, having a brother of a different colour was utterly irrelevant. In fact, he only realised Josh was a different colour when Gerhard was cuddling Katie. He kept moving around and looking at Gerhard and Katie from various angles before suddenly piping up, 'Is Katie a different colour?' Josh was standing beside him, and his immediate response was, 'Yes, she is adopted like me.' Mikey shot him a look and you could see the realisation on his face as he processed that Josh was also a different colour. It was one of those fascinating moments in the life of our family. But it would frustrate him so much if other kids asked questions. He couldn't understand why they would ask questions if he told someone that this was his brother. It made no sense to him at all.

He was eager to show Josh his classroom at one of his new schools. As he walked in with Josh, he introduced him to his classmates who were inside. 'This is my brother, Josh,' he said. He then became increasingly frustrated as he tried to show Josh different things while classmates kept interrupting, 'Your brother?' He thought it was completely ridiculous. He spoke English, and they understood it but still asked silly questions.

Katie's early years

When we dressed Katie, we noticed how incredibly distressed she would become if anything covered her face, even briefly. We realised that it might well be a trauma reaction to the fact that she had experienced a reduction in oxygen in the moments before she was born. We became cautious when dressing her, pulling no clothing over her head but placing her face through the clothing first and then pulling it over the back of her head. This kept Katie calm and relaxed while we dressed her.

Mikey learnt very quickly that if he wanted to hold his little sister, he needed to sit down and support her head. When he wanted to hold her, he would run to the couch, sit down, and raise both his hands almost horizontally – one to hold her and the other to support her head. That was his sign he was waiting for Katie to be placed in his arms. When Katie was sitting with us, Mikey loved reading to her. He read her all sorts of stories, mostly holding the books upside down as he read, more like turned the pages while creating his own story.

We would drop Josh at school every morning and then head over to Mikey's creche. Mikey refused to just say goodbye to his sister – it needed to be done properly. Katie and I would have to go into his classroom with him. He would put his bag down, quickly sit on the floor and raise his arms so that he could hold his sister. He would hold her so carefully and gently kiss her goodbye on her forehead while telling his friends, who automatically sat cross-legged next to him, "Don't touch, she is my sister." Thankfully, he reached a point where his friends could touch her hand or her cheek, but only he could hold her. He was such a protective brother and loved his little sister.

Josh spent ages lying next to Katie while she slept with his hand on her head, just looking adoringly at her. I discovered him one morning with the baby pouch strapped to his front. We carefully placed Katie into it, and she went straight to sleep with her brother gently patting and kissing her on top of her head. He displayed such nurturing and care.

Shortly after Katie came home, I was putting her to sleep, and Gerhard arrived home to find four-year-old Mikey on our carport roof. To say he was a busy kid was an understatement. Mikey decided early on to introduce Katie to play. While she was a few months old, sitting peacefully in her pram, he placed a plastic sword in her hand. With a sword in his hand, he readied himself for a sword fight. I told him Katie doesn't know how to sword fight and he said, 'Yes, she does' and proceeded to gently hit her sword with his as she sat there and giggled as her sword moved around in her hand.

I used to sing to Katie every time I changed her nappy and soon, we had a specific song that I sang repetitively and learnt as she grew older.

I'm a special girl,

Precious as can be,

My name is Katie Grace

And God loves me!

We still sing this song together when we are cuddling, in the car, or at random times when we are together and need to connect. Granny and her cousins would hold her hands at the beach and jump the waves while singing this song with her as she grew older.

Katie grew up with me 'lullabying,' but instead of falling asleep, she began to 'lullaby' with me! This tiny little girl was only just learning to talk. It was so beautiful!

Katie at school

Katie was so anxious when she was little. Loud noises were harsh for Katie to cope with. If the dogs barked in the house next door, she would throw herself onto the ground and cover her ears. I had to 'rescue' her from preschool one morning when the class listened to different animal sounds, and she just started crying and couldn't be consoled. I was anxious about her going into Grade 0 at her new primary school with class noises and teachers raising their voices.

Luckily, Katie had a superb teacher for Grade 0. With her anxiety still being so high by the end of the year, we decided to let her repeat her Grade 0 year to build her confidence while also hoping that her anxiety would subside. She had no issues being dropped off at school but would get anxious at the end of the day that we would not fetch her. No matter how often I told her that she was so special and that I would never forget to fetch her, this anxiety persisted. It was over this same time that Katie had recurring nightmares of being lost and not being able to find us or seeing us in the distance and us driving away without seeing her as she ran towards us. These dreams were disturbing to her and us as we managed them and talked them through with her.

By the time Katie got to Grade 1, she had grown in confidence. If her teacher raised her voice at anyone in the class, she would no longer fall apart, but her eyes would get watery. By Grade 2, she had learnt to hold her own and did not take teachers' raising their voices to heart. Her anxiety was much more under control than previously.

Katie began to realise that she did not always get the instruction from her teacher, as she often drifted off with other thoughts in class. Instead of asking her teacher to repeat an instruction, she created a successful plan. As the children's desks were separated, she couldn't easily see what another classmate was doing. She would, therefore, walk over to another child's desk and ask to borrow a specific pencil crayon. She explained that she had more time to figure out what she was supposed to be doing while her classmate searched for that particular colour. How did such a previously anxious child create such a plan?

This timid little girl has grown into a beautiful young lady. Her timidness has gone and has been replaced by a confident, caring person with an incredibly quick sense of humour and a deep sense of empathy. She doesn't miss a beat and can respond with lightning speed in a teasing conversation. She has an incredible EQ and will go out of her way to check that others are okay, including children who have previously been mean to her. She doesn't hold grudges, forgives easily, and never writes anyone off, as she believes everyone can change and that everybody makes mistakes sometimes. Such a beautiful gift she is to us and everyone around her! Did I mention that she has very strong opinions and often argues with her mom's opinion? She is bright, intelligent and opinionated!

One afternoon, Katie took the wind out of our sails. Her Dad had raised his voice at her. She calmly put up her hand and using words she had learnt from her brothers told her Dad to 'Calm his farm!' In absolute shock, Gerhard had to turn around so that she couldn't see him laughing. This was our anxious child!

Although Katie's anxiety is so much less than when she was little, the quickest way to trigger her anxiety is to raise your voice at her. This can be complicated in a big family when we sometimes want things to happen quickly. We see this in extra murals, especially those she is good at. It is the tendency of many coaches to raise their voices as competition time/exam time approaches. This doesn't improve Katie's performance; instead, it freezes it. Being shouted at makes her feel that she is in trouble and that she has done something wrong and then she just wants to apologise to make the shouting go away. One needs to talk gently and calmly to Katie to get the most out of her.

Katie – our princess from day one

Katie's creativity and determination is incredible. If she needs something or has an idea to make or create something, she gets up and does it. She makes what she needs and then plays with it. She does not bother about perfectionism, just practicality. She used cardboard to create the most stunning Barbie pizza shop. At one stage during play, we had to pause for coloured pieces of paper to be placed on the floor. She explained that this was for customers to keep their social distance. She also made Barbie clothes out of socks, scraps of material, paper and playdough. In her creative world, everything is possible.

Her fascination with horses has led her to create paddocks, farms, and horse-riding competitions. Then, one day, she decided she needed to make saddles and bridles for her horses. She made these with intricate detail using fabric. Even the stirrups were adjustable. They were all made to size so they would fit her horses perfectly.

Anything that disappears from the house can usually be found in Katie's bedroom – probably having become an integral part of a new play. At one stage, we searched everywhere for our dental floss, which was seemingly misplaced. We discovered it became a handbag for Barbie. This meant every time anything appeared lost or misplaced in the house, we would ask Katie where it was or look for it in her bedroom. It frustrated her, but we just about always found what we were looking for in her bedroom.

She has the most incredible rhythm. She cannot hear music without bursting into dance. She is constantly active and moving about with handstands, dance moves, poses, etc. It is unbelievable how quickly she can learn the steps of a dance online and then hum the tune to herself while replicating the dance beautifully for us.

I find it fascinating that people often talk about children not seeing colour. In my experience, children do see colour. The difference is they don't make colour an issue. On our way to school one morning, Katie blurted out with a cheeky smile, "You are so lucky you did not get a white daughter born out of your tummy, because she would have had hair like yours and she also would not be able to do it like you cannot do yours! You would have missed out on so much if you did not have this black face in your life." I just love her self-confidence and the knowledge that she is so loved.

When Katie and I walk hand in hand – which we still do at 12 years old – either one of us will squeeze the other's hand, immediately signalling the message 'I love you,' and the other responds with a hand squeeze. It's a beautiful, private form of communication shared between the two of us.

Katie has been a blessing and a joy to raise, just like her brothers. She was our princess from day one and continues to be. As a little girl, Katie was very timid and so tiny that you could just pick her up and cuddle with her. At twelve years old and with no more timidness, she is still small enough for us to pick her up and cuddle her. We have laughed a few times about me perhaps being the only mom who still picks up and cuddles her twelve-year-old.

Can you believe it? I was showing Katie a photo of my Grade 2 class. Her comment was, "There is no colour in your class.

Where is the beauty?" There was nothing wrong with her self-esteem or her ability to notice how white our class was.

Katie is extremely generous with her love, observing and including children who are alone. She once had a party with her friends at a public garden and noticed a child who arrived alone. It would have been so easy to continue playing with her friends, but she immediately included this child she did not know. She is always considerate and concerned about how others might be feeling.

Katie recently told us she wants to be rich one day but not so rich that she cannot see 'the hand of God move.' We have often used this terminology as we chatted about how much easier it is to see the miracles God performs when we have to rely on him. Very frequently, when people have enough, they may forget about their reliance on God as they feel they are fully able to provide for themselves. This leaves them in the unfortunate position of not always being able to recognise the miracles God performs daily.

I have always joked about praying for a rich husband and being specific in what we pray for. I planned to have a rich husband so we could travel the world together. Instead, God blessed me with a husband who was rich in spirit. As Gerhard and I were chatting about finances, Katie walked past us and piped up "I'm going to be specific when I pray!" She has a great sense of humour.

NAVIGATING FAMILY DYNAMICS

Coping with the Covid pandemic

This was a tough time for most people — a time of real fear and anxiety, but also a time of parents suddenly becoming homeschool teachers. With our children at different schools and each school adapting differently to the unfolding crises, we had various expectations that needed to be met. Katie couldn't understand why she had to attend a writing school – writing words and sentences, solving math problems, practising cursive writing, completing comprehensions, and doing other language exercises. Mikey's school on the other hand gave him experiments to complete. He had to drop different things from a height and record those that fell fastest to slowest, make music using stones, build a structure out of magnets and make elephant toothpaste.

Katie felt she was in the wrong school and would participate with Mikey in all his experiments. High school was quite different. Josh's teachers spent much of Covid speaking to walls. He would access the classes, turn off the picture and volume and face the computer to the walls. Fortunately, his teachers didn't feel the rejection, I don't think, as his screen was off.

Granny and Grandpa are integral to our children's lives, and they missed them terribly during Covid. Besides not wanting to make them sick, the retirement homes also closed access to everyone who didn't live there to keep the residents safe. We would take our trailer with chairs, biscuits, and hot water and park outside the village where we would unpack the chairs in the cul-de-sac and place them at safe distances from one another. Granny and Grandpa would come out to meet us at a safe distance with their cups of coffee, and we could connect, touch base, share stories and keep updated about our lives. Our children were such troopers. They missed our weekly Sunday lunches and jumped at any opportunity to have contact with their grandparents.

As Covid rules began to be lifted, Katie and I were able to visit Granny and Grandpa with a picnic blanket. We shared a social-distance tea party using Katie's China tea set. In that way, Katie was able to engage in 'play' with them in a safe way.

Early one morning, Katie woke with a low-grade temperature. As I was working with children, I could not take the risk of possibly infecting anyone, so we had Katie tested for Covid. She tested positive! We had been so cautious – and yet she was infected. The temperature had gone, and she had no further symptoms, but needed to be isolated in her room for ten days. I was keenly aware of her feeling rejected or traumatised by this event, so we turned it into a game called Hotel! Hotel! She could order room service whenever she wanted, and it would be delivered to her. Thankfully, she ordered less room service as the novelty died.

Josh and his high school 'drivers'

Having white parents was more manageable in primary school as everyone knew from the beginning with parents of primary school children being more present at schools, compared to children being more independent once reaching high school. Now and again, we would hear about incidents that happened and how well Josh handled himself. He was asked once why his brown mom never brings him to school and he responded 'God gave me a white mom. Do you have a problem with that? Posing that question at the end of his sentence ensured that no one asked any further questions.

High school was different. Josh chose to attend a school with only two children who knew him from primary school. This meant that none of the children were aware of his adoption. He absolutely loved his new school and slotted in very quickly with children he identified with physically. He would come home with comments like, "Now I know why I love chicken so much, all black people like chicken!" He really started forming his sense of self at this point. He had always been proud of being black, ever since he played tennis in primary school with a white child who 'went pink' from the heat during the game. He was not very impressed with people being pink and was grateful heat did not make him change colour.

Fetching him from high school became challenging for him as his friends asked who the white lady was who fetched him from school. He apologised the moment he climbed into the car one day explaining what the children asked him and apologising that his response was that I was his driver. With both Mikey and Katie in the car with me most afternoons, it would have been very believable to his friends. The following day, he left school with a huge smile, telling me about the kids who thought he came from a wealthy family because his parents could afford a white driver. We had to have a few conversations about being honest with friends because the longer we carry a lie, the more difficult it will be to navigate our way out of it.

Josh arrived home from school one day saying he really liked the name Sihle. We realised this might be part of his need to identify with his group of friends. We chatted about the name Simphiwe, one of the names we considered giving him when he first came home, which means 'gift'. He said he really liked that name too.

After Covid, he started at a new school. As the register was being called out, children were making the teachers aware of their nicknames. Thinking on his feet as he usually does, when his name was called, he told them he was known as Simphiwe. This added another round of humorous adjustments to our lives. The first time was a phone call from school. "Simphiwe is not well; please can you fetch him?" After my confused response, the caller clarified, "Your son!" I'm unsure what she thought of a mother who did not recognise her son's name.

Now we had to navigate being 'drivers' and having a child with two names depending on whether we were talking to him around people he had previously known or people from his new school. On one such day my husband went to fetch him from a new friend's house but had to clarify on his way there; "Am I Dad or the driver?" and "Are you Josh or Simphiwe?" It is essential to eliminate confusion by clarifying who you are and who you are fetching. We certainly had a few laughs with him around it.

People energise Josh. and He is incredibly social. He is such a joy to us, although he has also brought a fair amount of stress to us, always keeping us on our toes. This young man turns twenty-one this year.

Mikey is always up to something!

When Mikey started high school, he attended a small cottage school where he could get the academic support he needed. Due to his dyslexia, his subjects were all in different grades, so his schooling options were very limited.

At fifteen, he was offered an apprenticeship at a security company fitting electric fences, gate motors, security cameras, and security systems. This is Mikey's second year in the apprenticeship, and he is excelling. The anxiety has gone, the enthusiasm for learning is alive and well, and his self-esteem is flourishing. Indeed, he was not a schoolboy!

Josh often shakes his head at Mikey's actions with a massive smile spread across his face. Mikey absolutely fascinates him.

CULTIVATED BY LOVE

Precious family moments

Raising children is not for the faint-hearted. We adore our children and are so grateful for the miracle that each one of them is in our lives. Loving your children deeply does not make raising them any easier. We experienced many joyful and fun moments with our children, but we also experienced challenging and complex times that had us on our knees seeking guidance and direction from God.

Challenges are a part of life, but it is also tough as a parent needing to gently guide our children through challenges in their lives that cannot be removed, challenges that they needed to work through for themselves, with our support, while knowing we deeply and unconditionally love them.

One of the most beautiful conversations I recorded was when Mikey and Josh were chatting about how many children, they both wanted to have in the future. With a hint of concern in his voice, Mikey said, "What if I don't have a wife for babies to come out of?" and Josh's immediate response was; "Then you can adopt." It blows my mind that even as little children they have all been filled with so much compassion and are so aware of the needs of others around them.

As a teenager, Josh received his first paycheck for a Saturday job and immediately bought an air fryer for his grandparents because he overheard them chatting about buying one, and he wanted to surprise them. Mikey who saved money from his apprenticeship, noticed his grandparent's kettle was challenging to use as it did not separate from the base when they needed to fill it with water. He googled kettles, chose the one he wanted, and asked his Dad to run him down to the shops so that he could buy one for Granny and Grandpa.

Our children are not financially rich and were not raised in a wealthy home, but they have always had what they needed, even if they had to wait for and pray for it. All three of our children are rich in spirit. How blessed are we?

Our home is one where we express our love for one another daily and there is such a beautiful connection between all three siblings. They hug each other and verbalise their feelings. You might be in the kitchen making coffee or driving in the car when one of the children shouts out, "I love you, Mom, I love you, Dad, I love you, Josh, I love you, Mikey, I love you, Katie". We all do it, but it is so precious that teenage children do it so naturally. They constantly encourage one another and express pride when they achieve in any area.

Big children, big dreams, bright futures

Josh needs to be active and is adamant that he does not want to ever end up working behind a desk. He is so excited about leaving home to do an anti-poaching course and then work in one of the Big Five game reserves in South Africa for a year. I am so excited for him and his independence. Although I would prefer guns and 'baddies' not to be involved.

I must keep reminding myself what my father taught me – you love your children, educate them, and then set them free. I need to set Josh free to be the man he chooses to be. I cannot dictate what I want for him – which would be to wrap him in bubble plastic and keep him safe forever. Josh knows what drives him and makes him feel excited. He needs to follow his dreams and as parents, we need to guide and support him as we discuss his dreams and ideas for his life. We have to trust that what we instilled in him through the way he was raised, will always be with him as he makes decisions for his future.

Mikey has been offered a new apprenticeship which involves renovating steam trains. I have always had two black kids and a white one. Looks like I'm going to have three black kids now! He is super excited, and it sounds like such a great opportunity. Why as a mom can I not just be excited? While he was working with electric fences, I was concerned about him getting electrocuted. I'm now worried about the noise levels with the metal work and high-powered tools. I suppose it's the adage that a mom will worry about her children no matter how old they are.

Katie is in Grade 6 this year. She is happy and content, does as much work as necessary, and has a fantastic group of friends who have much fun together. She has recently started horse-riding lessons which she has wanted to do for ages. She thoroughly enjoys it and comes home on a high after every lesson. She does not worry about her future, but just enjoys every day as it comes.

She is a happy child who chats away eagerly and is so open about everything happening in her life at school, with her friends and feelings. For now, she does not cause me any worry in my life. Thank goodness for the four-year age gap I have between all my children.

I remember a friend asking whether I felt it was worth having children as she was undecided. I told her about the profound kind of love that will never be experience if one did not have children. There is also a lifetime of worry that accompanies parenting because of the depth of this love. I don't think I mentioned that part. I would not change having children for the world. It is so gratifying in so many ways.

Our kids' have self-confidence and love to laugh

I phoned Josh today to share some advice with him our black neighbour had given me. He said, "You see, always ask a black man." I said, "You are a black man, and you did not know the answer and he responded laughingly; "Yeah, but I'm a scam," making fun at the fact that he is a black child raised in a white family. He had a friend with him at the time but was still able to joke about himself. It fills me with such pride that he is so happy and content in his skin and that we were able to raise him so that he can love and value himself for who he is. As adoptive parents that is so often our concern. Will our children grow up focusing on what happened in their past and their history of being adopted or will they focus on their future recognising their value? Josh has amazed us with how well he has adjusted and grown.

Mikey was chatting at the dinner table about how he would also look black when he came home from working on steam engines, and Josh, who was about to head off into the bush on his anti-poaching course piped up; "Yeah, but I'm going to get even blacker, and yours will wash off." The boys constantly joke about colour and see themselves as being utterly equal because they are. They have a deep love for each other, but they also love teasing each other, jabbing each other with quick vocal antics about blackness and whiteness.

I have had to chat with them about the fact that what we find utterly normal in our home where we love and accept each other, could be misinterpreted by others in public. Mikey worded it so well; "I'm going to say something one day that someone is going to think is racist and I'm going to get 'klapped.' Outside of our home, others could take offence without realising the boys are brothers, and they, therefore, need to be careful about how they joke with one another when in public.

Mikey absolutely loves pap with gravy and recently tried eating it with his hand, which is how black South Africans often eat it. Josh has eaten it like this for a while, having been exposed to eating it this way by many of his friends. Mikey commented that maybe he is actually more black than white.

There was recently an incident at home when the door banged loudly. Katie jumped out of her chair and hid behind me. I said, "Go and open the door. It's just the wind". Katie responded, "No, I can't. I'm black; I'm too beautiful to die!"

On our way to church, Mikey commented that I was dressed all in black which is unusual for me as I mostly wear bright colours. I responded, 'I don't like being all in black' and Josh immediately retorted, 'You are such a racist.' He is so quick off the mark with his humour.

Josh mentioned to me the other day that he has a couple of friends who do not have great relationships with their mothers. He said the only thing he can really fault me on is that I love him too much! Gosh, I don't mind being faulted on that. It was the most fantastic compliment to receive from a twenty-year-old boy. It reminded me again about how incredibly blessed I am.

Josh knows who he is

People in the service industry have made it difficult for Josh by insisting on speaking only Zulu to him, even after he clarifies that he only speaks English and Afrikaans and can neither speak nor understand Zulu. This makes things more difficult for him and it is so unnecessary. This youngster has already faced adversity in terms of adoption and being raised by white parents. Respect from people of his colour would make things much easier for him.

Josh, of course, takes this in his stride. But it isn't something that he should have to deal with. It's interesting that he experienced more difficulties from white people when he was younger and more difficulties from black people now that he is grown up. Fortunately, Josh laughs off this ridiculousness. Josh does not allow other people's attitudes to steal from his self-esteem and the knowledge of who he is.

YOUTHFUL PERSPECTIVE

A village is needed to raise children

We often talk about how we need a village to raise children. We have been so incredibly blessed that, over time, familiarity has solved issues that initially existed, and our children have grown up being loved by two sets of grandparents and by all their aunts and uncles. It has been incredible to see this, and such a wonderful blessing as children need more than just moms and dads to grow and flourish as people. As grown children, our kids will voluntarily contact their grandparents and other relatives to play sports or meet up for a milkshake or breakfast. They will see things while shopping that they choose to buy for an aunt, uncle or grandparent as it makes them think of that person. We are so grateful to everyone in our family and our community as people have stepped up, loved and guided our beautiful children and built them into their lives.

This has resulted in some humorous incidents, too. Josh recently went to a private trainer and told him his aunt had recommended him. The trainer kept looking at Josh and repeating his aunt's name. Josh then realised the trainer was struggling to make sense of the black man in front of him and the white aunt he knew well. Again, we are so grateful that Josh experiences these incidents as humorous and not hurtful. It reminds me again how thankful we are for our children's positive self-esteem. None of them are pompous or proud, but each of them recognises their value as unique and loved individuals.

When we become so familiar with each other as people, we stop seeing colour and see the person instead. This was so wonderfully portrayed when a family member asked me in which hospital I gave birth to Josh, as they just could not remember having visited us in the hospital.

Josh's perceptions of growing up in a multicultural family

Josh said, "It was fun" when asked how he experienced growing up in our family. He went on to say, "White people's activities are enjoyable like camping and stuff which black people don't do as much. It is also fun because we get to joke around a lot about colour without it being offensive" He said that when he was still in primary school, it was difficult because children would ask him so many questions about having white parents. Yet, it was normal for him to have white parents and different-coloured siblings.

Mikey's perceptions of growing up in a multicultural family

When asked what it felt like growing up in our family, Mikey said it was exciting and entertaining. When I asked him what it felt like being different from his siblings, he responded, "What do you mean?" I clarified that his siblings are both adopted and black, and he replied, "Just because they are a different skin colour does not mean they are not my brother and sister."

Katie's perceptions of growing up in a multicultural family

When I asked Katie about her perceptions of growing up in our family she said "It's fun! It's fun, being different and being around people of different colour". When asked about her brothers, she said it is really normal having two brothers of different colours. She does not notice it as she just knows her brothers as the people they are.

She did say that it is frustrating having white parents who can't help her with her hair – nor that her mom could not have helped a white child with her hair either. She also finds it a bit embarrassing when in a shopping mall someone speaks to her in a language she does not understand, as she does not know what to say.

EPILOGUE

Nothing we do ever changes God. We allow our picture of God or our God image to change. We change the way we see God because of the pain or difficulties we experience, instead of holding firmly to our belief that through good and bad seasons in our lives, God always remains the same. He is our only constant, and God is always good. God has journeyed with me in my infertility and taken me from a place of feeling like a second-rate mom to being a good mother. "To God be the Glory for great things He has done."

I am so proud of our 'post-apartheid' family – English, Afrikaans, black and white. Love is alive and well and crosses all barriers. We either teach our children to love unconditionally or not to. Teaching our children to only love some people equates to them never learning to love unconditionally. We all strive to be loved unconditionally, so why do we struggle so much to show this love to others? Do our family notice differences? Yes. Do we sometimes highlight differences? Yes. But this is to celebrate them. As we celebrate them, we develop a sense of community and belonging. We celebrate each one of our children in their uniqueness. What a privilege and a gift to be parents.

RESOURCES

NIV Bible

Good News Bible. 1982. pg. 241

RBC Discovery Series: Why would a good God allow suffering?

Moore, B. 1999. Breaking Free. Lifeway Press, Nashville, Tennessee

ACKNOWLEDGEMENTS

Thank you to:

~ Vic Graham for taking the time to pen his thoughts to us after our time with him was over.

~ Ann Rundle and Marge Stathakis for the preparation and time they put into the material for the retreat which gave me massive insight into myself and helped with my healing process.

~ Dennis Beeselaar from whom I first learnt about how we create God images based on our life experiences.

www.ingramcontent.com/pod-product-compliance
Lightning Source LLC
Chambersburg PA
CBHW052051220426
43663CB00012B/2531